Shovelhead Redemption:

The Ride Back from Hell

Abby Clabough

ISBN: 0615530281

ISBN-13:978-0615530284

Biker Chick Books

bikerchickbooks.com

Thanks to everyone who is a part of this story. My greatest believers - Cheryl, Amy, Brenda, Mom and the guys from Bike-Talk - you guys rock. Gigi, I appreciate your superior editing skills (in addition to your quick jaunt up to NH); I was so sick of looking at this. Rick's editing too, if only so you can throw this back in Brenda's face on a bar stool at Bruce's. The most important person in my life is Dan, who made the story possible, even though he broke the medium bowl and didn't tell me. I wouldn't have made the tough choices if I hadn't wanted a better life for him. I'm not sure if he'll ever understand how much I love him.

Table of Contents

Prologue

It's been a particularly long psychotic break, starting on Superbowl Sunday, and here it is, the middle of June. I've carefully chosen every spoken word, picked no battles, and have made sure he's asleep before I dare shut my eyes. I rush home from work every day so I won't be accused of cheating, while my heart skips a beat when I pull in the long dirt driveway wondering what brand of insanity I'll be facing when I walk in the door.

I mention to him that a friend wants me to babysit for her kids tomorrow. I don't know why this particular statement is so offensive, but when you're dealing with someone for whom logic is not a reality, there usually is no reason. Not one that makes sense in my world.

I see the flowered wallpaper in the budget mobile home's bathroom. I see the large mirror mounted on the wall. I see the small shelves I've covered with contact paper and hung over the vanity. I see the 9mm pistol loaded with 19 rounds of hollow point ammunition, and one in the chamber, pointed at my head. There is always one in the chamber.

"You have a problem. Your parents hypnotized you when you were young, and they pimped you out."

What? My childhood was not one of great love and happiness. My father was a mean drunk, and my mother never seemed to care, but they certainly did not hypnotize me or sell me to... who? The other lawyers, doctors and CEOs at our golf and yacht clubs?

"What are you talking about? My parents would never do anything like that."

"They did, and you don't remember because you were hypnotized."

"Well how do you know about it?"

Wrong question, because again, logic has no place in his world. I start thinking about the man at our church whose brother committed a murder-suicide, killing his wife and children and then himself. Suddenly I understand how this shit happens. Suddenly I understand that of course mothers who drown their children are insane. Normal people don't do that. I'm not only worried about my life, but what will happen to my son sleeping in the bedroom that shares a wall with the bathroom.

Glossary

If you aren't a biker, there might be a few terms you don't understand. Hopefully this will help.

Shovelhead – A Harley-Davidson engine made from 1966 through 1984.

Panhead – Harley-Davidson engine made from 1948 through 1965.

Suicide Clutch – Clutches on older Harleys were operated with the foot and had hand shifters. It's called a "Suicide" clutch because it's tricky to use.

Basket Case – A collection of motorcycle parts that make up a whole bike but aren't assembled.

One percenter – it is generally thought that the origin of the term comes from the American Motorcyclist Association's statement that 99% of motorcycle riders are law-abiding citizens , leaving the other 1%... not so much.

1

I don't remember exactly when I decided I was going to be a biker chick, but it was a decision. I didn't fall into it because I met a biker. I looked for bikers. Maybe it was the era, but it never occurred to me that I could go to school, get a job, and simply buy a Harley-Davidson. For some reason I felt I had to get there through someone, through an existing biker. Perhaps it was because I wanted the lifestyle as much as the motorcycle.

Why was the lifestyle so attractive when I was born into a life that included ski homes, country clubs and private schools? Alcoholism. In hindsight, I can confidently take it down to that one word. My parents were Ivy League educated, from good families and acted as though the worst thing in our lives was a bad golf game or a wipe-out on the slopes. There was no swearing or yelling or any manner of displaying emotion toward each other. We were devoid of any feelings except distaste, ridicule and apathy – a complete lack of feelings.

It's possible that my brothers, who are six and nine years older than me, had a different experience. I never felt like I was at home or fit in anywhere. When my brothers teased and humiliated me, my mother just told me to ignore them. She was raised in a household where ladies didn't get angry or express displeasure. You just smiled and pretended nothing bothered you. I don't think I smiled much, and I don't think anyone was fooled, but the men in my family kept letting me know how useless I was. It could be that my brothers got the same treatment from my father, and the shit was rolling down hill. Problem was, I was at the bottom of the heap, so it all piled up on me.

My father didn't beat us other than a spanking when we screwed up, but he was just a plain old asshole when he was drunk. If I had been an adult, I would have known that alcohol was the problem. As a kid, there's only one reason why people treat you badly, and that's because you deserve it. I guess I handled it by figuratively telling them all to go fuck themselves and became an alcoholic young woman that hung out with dirt bags.

What made me think that the biker's lifestyle of the seventies and eighties was any different than our cold home? Perhaps because it appeared to be the complete opposite of our world. It was too bad we couldn't have been a family of Irish Catholic drunks who all had a great time getting sloshed together, fighting a common enemy, and standing beside each other to the end. We were the uptight

WASPs who snuck off to our dark corners to drown our miseries in solitude.

Regardless of the lack of sense it makes now, I was determined that the outcast biker life was the path for me. I fought to leave private school for public school and immediately got in with the group of losers who were skipping classes and smoking and drinking under the platform at the train station. Where I'd been winning awards for scholarship and athletics in the elitist academy hidden behind stone walls, I quickly became the girl that people didn't want their kids hanging around with.

I had a crush on a total loser in junior high. I'd get detention on purpose if I knew he'd be there. We connected, and he came over to the house one day. The next day, my brother's car was missing. The juvenile delinquent I brought home had stolen the keys when he was in the house and returned later to steal it. As I had learned in life, I pretended it didn't bother me. At least I had enough sense to stay away from the guy after that.

By the time I was 14, I was drinking in bars, fighting, getting myself in really bad situations, and working my way onto the back seat of a Harley, any Harley. I just wanted to be on a bike.

I finally landed a real biker boyfriend. A nice Italian boy with an ego and a temper. One who eventually beat and raped me for hours one night after I'd beaten him at a game of pool. I didn't go home for days so my parents couldn't see me, but once again, I had enough sense to stay away from him after that.

My next biker boyfriend was a much better catch. He was a tough guy, but he was more the strong and silent type, and although he had to keep my drunken ass in line from time to time, he was a good guy. However, my parents insisted I go to college somewhere, anywhere, away from home, and I never saw Danny again.

But I had a strategy. My father had been trying to get me interested in flying airplanes. There was a university in Daytona Beach that trained students to become pilots. There were bikers in Daytona Beach. I could actually get my parents to fund my immersion in the biker haven.

It wasn't long before I was frequenting the Boothill Saloon and other biker dives in Daytona Beach. I wasn't too discriminating. I just wanted to party and ride. I met a guy from Atlanta and we worked out a deal to trade my Camaro for a Sportster and a Shovelhead. Soon we became romantically involved. Jimmy was easily the most unattractive man I'd ever laid eyes on, but he was fun and funny and had lots of drugs. And he could get me onto my own Harley-Davidson.

The deal Jimmy and I made was to trade an old hard tail (no rear suspension) Sportster and a Shovelhead for my bare bones '78 Camaro. Jimmy was making out on the deal, but I didn't care. I just wanted a Harley. I went to Atlanta to learn how to ride the motorcycle and get it back to Daytona.

2

I started learning to ride in Jimmy's neighborhood, which consisted of a looped road with a stop sign at the top of a steep hill. It wasn't pretty. I know I went down a few times, but the most memorable was when I hit a tree in someone's yard after trying to start out from the stop sign. The carburetor was knocked off the bike, and I'd slammed my chest into the end of the handlebar somehow. The next day we went to a parking lot with one of Jimmy's friends to help out. I finally figured it out and rode the Sportster back to Daytona with Jimmy riding alongside me.

What should have been an eight hour trip took three days. First there was the fact that the carburetor kept falling off. We hadn't found the right clamps to put the Tillotson back on after the run-in with the tree. Radiator clamps were used. They'd work for about fifty miles, then I'd hear the engine racing, and it was time to stop and reinstall the carburetor. This was especially fun considering how hot the engine was to the touch.

Adding to the excitement was what must

have been a cracked sternum for me - also from the tree incident. Once I got moving in the morning, I was OK, but I'd have to roll out of bed, getting my feet to the floor and gingerly standing upright. Coughing, sneezing, and laughing were extremely painful for months.

Despite the challenges of the ride, this is when I started falling for Jimmy. He was a very funny guy and seemed to know everyone. Not only did he know people, but they all liked him. No matter where we were on the 450 mile trip, Jimmy knew someone at the most critical times. These people always seemed happy to see him, and I thought that was indicative of a real stand-up guy.

We made it to Daytona, but it wasn't long before I decided to make a change. I showed up at Jimmy's doorstep with everything I owned. I didn't tell my parents I'd left school and Daytona. In her search, my mother called the Boothill Saloon looking for me. One of the bartenders grabbed the phone number of the bike shop Jimmy worked at off of a t-shirt hanging on the wall, and my mother tracked me down.

Jimmy had often rambled on about how much he cared for me and about opening a bike shop together in the mountains, and I thought it sounded like a great idea. When I showed up unannounced, Jimmy could have told me to get lost, but he didn't. In hindsight, I think he viewed my family as a source of cash. Everything Jimmy did was related to a deal, and I was no exception.

Life was a combination of visiting with the few people that did come to the shop, parties, small trips, and swap meets. A little over a year into it, we got married. Through the three years we were together, I got to ride a variety of Harleys, but there were none that were truly mine. If someone was interested in buying the bike I was on, it was theirs. They were bikes that Jimmy would buy or we'd build and then soon after completion they were gone. I never did see the Shovelhead I was promised, and the Sportster was sold early on.

We tried to create a successful business, but we were living in part of the most notorious backwoods country in the south. Not a lot of bikers. Also, this was back at the start of the eighties when Harley riders were not liked or wanted. The locals constantly tried to find ways to get rid of us.

When the shop got broken into late one night, the local police were kind enough to drive to our home about 10 miles away and bring us to the station to file a report. Jimmy thanked them a couple of times, telling them it was very considerate of them to help us out like that. They took Jimmy into a separate room to discuss the break-in. It seemed odd, but nothing was typical in those parts. When Jimmy came out, he told me not to worry. I hadn't expected to be worried, which of course caused me to worry.

When I entered the room, there was a man with his arm in a cast sitting in the corner. No introductions were made. The officer told me why I was there.

"When we discovered your shop had been broken into, we took a look around to see what damage had been done."

"OK."

"We found a baggie filled with a white powdery substance in the desk drawer."

"Uh, yeah. That's salt."

The man in the cast, who was finally introduced as an agent from the Georgia Bureau of Investigation office about two hours away, shook his head in frustration. It was 2:00 in the morning, and the injured guy had driven all that way for a bag of salt. I can't tell you why we didn't have a salt shaker, but apparently the locals expected salt to be in salt shakers in their town. Fortunately storing salt in a baggie wasn't a crime, and the cops took us home.

The cops weren't all wrong, and neither were the locals. Jimmy was a drug dealer, but he was careful not to do anything locally. It caught up to him eventually.

I didn't have much contact with my family

for a long time. Jimmy didn't have a lot going on with his family either. Holidays were always spent with friends, usually friends who weren't close to their families, geographically or emotionally. On Thanksgiving in 1982, we were at our little house in the woods with Crazy Dave, Billy, Janice, and Janice's son. I was suffering from allergies and had taken something that knocked me out. I woke up when someone pounded on the bedroom door and announced that federal agents had shown up and arrested Jimmy.

I was stunned. I expected that I was going to be hauled away too, but it quickly became clear that they had no interest in me. They really wanted Jimmy's bike. The feds were searching the chicken house and the root cellar and under every log, but they didn't think to look on the back porch where Jimmy always parked. They took me to the shop to open it up so they could look for Jimmy's Panhead there. There was a bike, but the local cop confirmed my story that it belonged to a customer. Small town.

After the feds left town with Jimmy, I went back to the house and immediately started disassembling Jimmy's bike to send to a friend's house. I thought it would be really hard for anyone to identify the basket case as the bike the feds were looking for, although they probably had a vehicle identification number from his registration.

At the time, Jimmy was wrapped up in a

bunch of deals with Al. I really liked the guy. He had everything figured out. Al seemed to have unlimited resources. Perhaps being a successful businessman is what intrigued me about him. Jimmy was well known for "robbing Peter to pay Paul." His deals were always made with credit on both the front and the back end. What that meant was that Jimmy always owed money, and people always owed him. Deal A might happen on one day, and by the time he got paid for it, Deal B would pop up, but cash only. So Deal A's money would be given to the vendor of Deal B, keeping the Deal A person on hold while Deal B got completed and more money was made (theoretically) than would have been made otherwise. It was a crazy web of debt, and there was no end.

Al had cash. Al had bulletproof vests and ammunition and all kinds of cool stuff. Jimmy was going to be out of town for one of the big swap meets, so I went and set up our booth with a girlfriend. I was able to get a space next to Al, who sold boots and leather vests. I met Al's girlfriend, and although I've never been very knowledgeable about glamour, it was obvious to me that she was wearing a wig. I couldn't figure out why a woman would wear a wig if it wasn't going to be attractive. It all made sense after Jimmy got out of jail and told me that they had photos of him meeting Al in a rest area. Al was a federal agent. I felt betrayed.

Things changed after that. We moved to

another part of the state that was more conducive to motorcycle sales and repair. I picked up a job as a stripper. I accompanied Jimmy to his first appearance in Federal court, which is when I learned something about the man I'd married. He'd always drilled into me that you never snitch on anyone. You get busted; you take the consequences. You should make enough on the deal to pay the lawyer. We weren't five minutes in the office with the agent before Jimmy ratted someone out. They wanted club members; Jimmy didn't give them any. I don't know that there was anything he could even tell them about the club. Jimmy threw the feds a bone, but it wasn't the one they were looking for. The name Jimmy gave them wasn't enough to cut him any deals, and maybe it was small potatoes to all of them, but I was sick to my stomach and left the building immediately.

I don't know what Jimmy told them after that, and I never asked. I realize that I was not the one facing prison time. But I also know what he drilled into me, and while I would have been terrified about going to jail, I don't think I would have snitched on anyone, even if it was out of fear more than loyalty. What burns me about it is that he did that to me so that if I got busted, I wouldn't give him up. The irony of the situation was that it was just one more lousy deal he made. Eventually Jimmy went to jail, leaving behind a lot of unpaid debts and pissed off drug dealers.

One of those drug dealers was a guy who had provided the goods for one of Jimmy's deals with Al. He'd gotten in a jam when the DEA flew over his crops and he thought that shooting at them was a good idea. The grower had managed to hide a few pounds from the Feds, and he gave it to Jimmy to sell for him. I begged Jimmy to do a cash-only deal when he went out of town with it. But no, Jimmy traded for a different product, which he then gave to Al for future payment. All $15,000 of it. The feds ended Jimmy's career before they paid him for the goods, and the grower never got his money.

There were a few people like this floating around. Unfinished deals. Jimmy was back in town for a while, so I don't know why these guys didn't start knocking on the door before he went to jail. We were drifting apart at that point. He'd promised when he left town with the weed that he'd come back with the money (rather than his usual twisted shenanigans), and he hadn't. Now the dealer wanted me to sign over my small house on the Tennessee-Georgia border to him. It wasn't much of a house, but I wasn't the one that gave away the farm. I left it up to Jimmy to figure out while I went to work at the strip club.

3

Ah yes. Stripping. Great money, no taxes, lots of partying - an awesome source of income as long as you don't mind taking your clothes off in front of strangers. This was incredibly awkward for me, but after Jimmy got busted, it was the best option even though I couldn't understand why anyone would want to see me naked. Becoming an exotic dancer is an awkward job for a modest, insecure, uptight preppie who has no clue how to dance in any capacity.

I take that back. I could dance. I was forced into ballroom dancing classes with the rest of the country club crowd when I was young. I was the tallest and least dainty person in the class. Probably the highest grades in school too. Pair those qualities with the fact that there was one more girl than there were boys in the class, and you can imagine how humiliating the whole situation was for me. While my brothers had been chipping away at my self-esteem for years, whatever was left was destroyed on the dance floor at the Pequot Library. So ten years later I knew how to dance, but not in a way that helped in my current situation.

What did help? Alcohol. Lots of alcohol. Give me a Black Russian. Vodka and Kahlua. No mixers in the drink at all. Liquid audacity so I could act like I wanted to hang out with some loser, make him think he'd get lucky, and free him of his hard-earned money.

As with any group that gets stereotyped, every chick I worked with had a different story, a distinct personality. Karen was a contortionist. She'd have the bartender turn the lights down low to hide evidence that she had a decade or two on most of us. She'd perform backbends and headstands and other gymnastics with only a g-string and then sit on the floor, cross-legged, and roll around topless. There was another woman, Peaches, who got kicked out of her home state of Florida. I think she caused an accident with the wrong person when she was drunk. I don't know the full details, but regardless, she couldn't go back. Jamie was an alcoholic who was court-ordered to take Antabuse, a drug that would make her violently ill if she drank. That didn't keep her from drinking every once in a while, and she was not a pleasant drunk.

The first club I worked at was unusual in that the dance floor was not a raised platform but a regular hardwood dance floor with small tables lining the edge. We danced a rotation, one girl on the main floor at a time. When the guys wanted to tip us, they'd wave a bill, and we'd come over and raise a gartered leg up to the edge of the table so they could slide the bill under the elastic. The table dances were how we made money. For $20 a guy could enjoy his own private show. Pretty simple. None of that lap dance stuff thankfully. We also sold drinks. We saved the little swords that came in the drinks, and we were paid a commission at the end of the night for each little plastic weapon we turned in.

It was while I was working at the strip club, and after Jimmy was sent to prison, that Buck stopped by the bar. I'd first met Buck a couple of years earlier when a group of us had been thrown in jail for no good reason. It was when Jimmy and I had the bike shop in its first location, in the middle of a small backwoods North Georgia town that wasn't enamored with its new biker residents.

There was a big biker party about 20 miles north of the shop with most people riding from the south. We thought it was a good opportunity to get some business, so we talked to one of the local cops who was younger and more forward-thinking than the others, and he said it would be fine if we had a keg in the shop as long as people weren't drinking outside. We thought everything was good, but when the bikes would roll into town in groups, the town leaders were horrified. They'd send cops down to run the bikers off. That group would leave, and a little later another group would roll in. Around noon, there was a group of seven of us hanging out inside the shop; three couples and one single guy known as Cardboard.

The friendly cop showed up and informed us that he'd been told to arrest us all. The guys pushed their bikes into the shop so we could lock them up before getting hauled off to jail. After the bikes were secured, the officer told us to get in the car. All seven of us. One car. We looked at the law man, wondering if he was going to take us in shifts, if we were expected to sit on laps, ride on the trunk, or what. More cars came, and we all sat in jail for several hours while they figured out what to charge us with.

There were four guys in one cell and three women in the other: Animal and his girlfriend, Crazy Dave and his wife, Jimmy and I, and Cardboard, who was a member of the (somewhat) local 1% club. When they were doing the necessary paperwork to check us in, they asked Cardboard what his name was. He told them. After that they referred to him as Mr. Board. That was probably the most entertaining incident of the day as we sat and waited, waited, waited until they let us go.

Finally someone came through the door and said that Mr. Board was getting bailed out. Finally some movement! Of course Cardboard needed to get his bike out of the shop, so they bailed me out. Why me and not Jimmy, I don't know, but I wasn't complaining. It was Buck and his wife Suzie, and we all drove back to the shop so I could unlock it and free Cardboard's bike. I returned for Jimmy, who in turn bailed out the next person, who bailed out the next person, and so on until we were all out of jail. It was getting late at this point, and we grabbed the bikes and headed up to the party.

That's how I met Buck. I saw him a few times over the next year or so at swap meets, always with his wife. It was about three days after Jimmy went to jail that Buck showed up at the strip club where I was working. Suzie had died a few days before. She'd been buried in South Carolina, and he was on his way back home after the funeral.

Having Buck around seemed like a good deterrent for all of Jimmy's creditors. Buck hung around town for a few days. We carried Mezcal in the saddlebags and would pick up some tacos and find a place to picnic, drink the smokey liquid, and burn a joint or two. After that I'd go to work. Buck went back to his life after that, but we kept in touch.

At the strip club, most of the patrons were local businessmen or farmers who came to the club a day or two a week. There were some folks from out of town, but it was a friendly place for a strip club. The bouncers had an easy job. That's why it was a surprise when I offered my leg for the tip being offered only to have the guy yank it back. Ha ha. Funny guy. I figured he was trying to get my attention with a harmless game, until he did it a second time. The third time I didn't bother giving the guy another glance. That's when he called me a slut. I can only imagine what it looked like to see a topless 21-year-old pick up a heavy glass ashtray and wing it at a guy's head. I suppose I was lucky it missed and bounced off the wall behind him, since the fucker was a cop. I got fired.

I told Buck what happened, and he suggested I move to his place and find a job at a bar in Atlanta. Even though I got a call back to the bar I'd been fired from, the threats from Jimmy's dealers were starting to get more frequent, and moving in with Buck was the perfect way to get them off my back. At Buck's request, I divorced Jimmy. I would have done it anyway. After Jimmy got busted, his true character had come out, and that person was far different from the man I thought I'd married.

I hit the bars looking for a job. In one downtown club, I was the only white woman. They wanted me to be a feature dancer, making $300 a night plus tips. It was a champagne bar, meaning I'd request a glass of champagne when a patron wanted to buy me a drink. They'd end up paying some absurd amount of money for a bottle of Champale. First of all, I didn't want to be in the minority, and I certainly didn't have enough skills to be a feature dancer. That would have required choreography, expensive costumes, poles and the ability to send tassels spinning in opposite directions at will. Selling Champale? Stripping is a sales job. You're pitching a fantasy that almost never gets realized. And while some think that being an exotic dancer is scraping the bottom, selling Champale was not a tool I was willing to use.

I had a few tattoos, so the glitzy downtown clubs were out. I found a job on the northern edge of downtown where there was a healthy convention business. Unlike my starter club, the main dance floor was a platform, a sheet of clear plastic over colored lights. The heat from the bulbs had caused the plastic to warp, which made dancing in spike heels six feet above the floor a special thrill. There was only one thing more exciting than dancing on the lights, and that was the table dance scenario.

We were required to stand on the tables to dance, with strict orders to keep our legs together. These were cheap cocktail tables - a single center leg with little to keep the table balanced. Thankfully there were tapestries draped across the ceiling, so we had something to hold onto. The support was purely psychological, because in the event that a girl tried to keep herself from falling by clutching the fabric ceiling, everything came tumbling down. So what was referred to as a table dance was really more of a table surf, trying to keep balanced without the ability to stabilize our footing for the duration of a song. I don't know why more guys didn't bust out laughing.

One night on my way to work at the club, I

stopped to get gas. I ran in quickly to pay, and when I returned to the truck, I found that my bag of costumes had been stolen.

Costumes are another unique part of the exotic dancing industry. Back in the day, the outfits were purchased from women who traveled from club to club, selling their wares. The costumes were made from stretchy materials with Velcro in strategic places and often fringe and sequins or rhinestones. While they were cheap in construction, they were expensive to purchase, and you never knew when the stripper costume sales lady was coming back. Losing a whole bagful was a huge blow.

With no work clothes, I rushed back home, stomped into the house and slammed the door. Before I could say that my costumes had been stolen, I was laid out on the floor and getting kicked in the back. I'd already been hit in the face and the stomach. I was told that I was never to slam his door again. If I didn't like it, I could leave, but everything I owned was staying behind, and he'd hunt me down and kill me. My options were limited.

I had known Buck expressed anger with his fists, but I hadn't known it would be so easy for him to flip on me. The door wasn't damaged, but I was. I called into work and told them I wouldn't be in, explaining the circumstances. My boss acted as though he'd heard this every day and told me to come in anyway. I didn't think I'd make much money with a black eye and swollen face, but he didn't care.

While Buck was a tough guy, he was also very intelligent. He was an experienced land surveyor who led crews and whose work was respected. He did have a temper and little tolerance for people who didn't act the way he wanted them to. But even in the middle of flattening some loser who figured Buck wasn't as tough as he looked, Buck was thinking straight. I could manage that situation. What I couldn't handle was what happened next.

4

Buck wasn't expressive, outside of pummeling someone. Even then, it wasn't so much that he was angry; it was more for sport. I think he liked it when someone gave him an excuse. When his wife died, he didn't act very upset. When we met up right after Suzie's death, he didn't appear to be grieving too much.

I moved in with Buck knowing very little about him. I didn't even know his last name. I did know that he had a son who was about two years old who was staying with Suzie's parents, but Buck didn't seem driven to get his son back. I was too clueless at the time to realize that wasn't normal, and I wasn't even considering the possibility of being a full time stepmother. Not too long after I moved in, Buck's mother died. That's when the fun began.

We headed to Tennessee for the funeral. Buck's mother had been married several times, and based on the statements Buck was making, I started to wonder if any of his stepfathers had molested him. The rantings were cryptic enough that I couldn't be sure. Buck had been raised in a church where they handled snakes, spoke in tongues and demons were part of everyday life and conversation. I was trying to put all of these pieces together to figure out where Buck's mind was. He was extremely paranoid about being at the funeral. It went downhill from there.

After the funeral is when life became very scary. Buck was sure his brothers (from the club) were out to get him. He'd left the club after several dedicated years when it was discovered that his son was born with a large hole in his heart and would need a lot of medical care. Buck, Suzie, and their son had moved to Atlanta to be near her parents and an excellent children's hospital. I never asked, but I speculate that although there was a chapter of the club in Buck's new hometown, his need for health insurance for his son meant a regular job. However it happened, Buck was no longer in the club, but he was still on good terms with his former club brothers.

I wasn't comfortable with the fact that Buck thought the club was out to get him. There was no good outcome to that situation. I wanted to ask someone for help, but I didn't feel it was possible. I couldn't trust anyone. It wasn't a one-way street though. I couldn't trust any of them because they couldn't trust me. Nobody knew me beyond just knowing who I was. One day I'd been at the clubhouse with Buck, and for some reason I was walking across the yard by myself. Buck's closest friend was there and asked if I'd come to the clubhouse by myself - and not in a very pleasant way. I don't know what his response would have been if I had come by myself, but I'm sure it would not have been good. There was no way I'd have gone alone at any point in time, and I wasn't about to show up there saying that Buck had lost his mind and was sure they were all out to get him. This left the few friends I had, none of whom were going to question Buck. And while I was desperate for help for Buck, what could anyone do?

After his mother's funeral, Buck and I embarked on a journey. It was non-stop, top-speed, and went through four states. It was in a pickup truck with a 12 gauge shotgun hanging in the back window and a handgun on the seat. Buck's sidearm of choice was a .44 revolver at that time. He was hunting demons, which came in many forms, and he was going to kill them when he found them. The scary part was that every time we stopped or a car passed us or someone glanced our way, the enemy was there. The shooting was going to start at any minute. Innocent people were going to die, and I had no idea what I could do to stop it.

At one point during the three-day, multi-state adventure, Buck brought the truck to a sudden stop, jumped out, and came back with a toy tomahawk he'd somehow spotted on the side of the road. The tomahawk was a secret weapon and was going to protect us from the demons. Later in the trip, I was extremely frustrated that my logic wasn't working with Buck, and I hit the dashboard of the truck with the toy. The head broke off the tomahawk and went spinning out the open window. Buck raged that I was working with the demons. It was a tense few moments, and I'm glad Buck was driving or the beating would have been a lot worse.

Demons were also the focus one night at a friend's house. Tim and Marjorie were a couple that I'd met through Jimmy. Tim had built a rustic home over time on the edge of a small city in northwest Georgia and was building a bike shop. We were visiting one weekend when Buck built a fire and proceeded to burn everything that was, in his mind, possessed by demons. Random garden tools, a robe with a picture of a dragon on it, anything that struck him as evil. Tim, Marjorie and I tried to find the right words that would quell the bonfire, but nothing short of shooting Buck was going to stop him.

Another time, Buck was pouring a line of oil around the perimeter of our home. When I asked him why he was doing that, he accused me of consorting with the demons and threatened me with a shotgun.

Of course I considered leaving, but I knew there was a man I wanted to be with in that warped mind somewhere. I didn't want to give up on him and leave when he was in need. I hung on for the ride and hoped that the insanity brought on by his mother's death would eventually subside – and that I'd live through it.

Buck received life insurance money from Suzie's death. We partied, we rode, we bought a piece of property in the woods of north Georgia. The 27 acre plot was remote and didn't have electricity or water at the time. The deed stated a right-of-way for utilities, but after the purchase we were told by the Amicalola Electric Membership Corporation that they couldn't run power to the property because they'd have to place the anchor for one guide wire outside of the existing right-of-way on an adjacent piece of property. There is more than one way to run a pole line, but they weren't budging, and nobody seemed inclined to help us. We'd have to get the owner of the land that stood between us and existing power to sign a right-of-way before we could get the lights turned on.

We were too committed to living on the property at that point, and we moved ahead with the construction of a small home. We placed some large beams in the ground as a foundation for a pole house. A 10 foot by 20 foot shed with a door and windows was built along with an open shed to house the motorcycle. Then we ran out of money.

Friends moved into Buck's house in the Atlanta suburbs, and we moved into the shed. We had a wood stove for heating and cooking, and all other appliances were made by Coleman. Coleman stove, Coleman lantern, Coleman coolers (for water and refrigeration), Coleman fuel. In the beginning we had a running pickup truck, so we were able to go into town to fill our water jugs at the gas station. There was a spring on the property, not too far from where the shed was located. It was down a fairly steep incline, so it was easy to get down there with the empty jugs; not so easy coming back up with the full ones.

We heated water on the stove for cleaning and cooking. We had to buy a bag of ice daily to keep fresh what little food we had in the cooler. Beans and rice were lunch and dinner. Eggs, as long as we could afford them, were easy to keep in the cooler as long as we could get them in a container that didn't disintegrate in the water left by the melting ice.

The shed was small, and there wasn't a lot to do. We existed. We rode to friends' homes for entertainment, showers, laundry and to smoke their weed. Buck's psychosis seemed to be mellowing out, especially when he could get a buzz. I hated riding around to various homes looking for a joint to smoke, but it was a tranquilizer for his tortured mind.

My birthday rolled around, and maybe the word "birth" caused the gears to turn in Buck's head. Suddenly he was convinced that we should have a baby with a fervor that scared me. I went along with his determination to make one right then and there, because really, what were the chances?

Birthday. Birthdays. I had a few memorable birthdays back in the day. That happens when you drink too much. Any excuse is a good one.

On my 20th birthday I was living with Jimmy, hanging out with our friend Jeff while Jimmy was off somewhere selling drugs. Jeff and I were kicking back, smoking some weed. For some reason, known only to people who smoke pot and come up with similar bright ideas, I decided to show Jeff my new shotgun.

The shotgun was not a typical configuration. It was a pump with an external hammer – probably a Winchester 1897. It was old and in rough shape. When I was done showing it to Jeff, I loaded it and put a shell in the chamber. Putting a shell in the chamber meant pumping it, which meant the hammer was cocked. It was now necessary to carefully lower the hammer. Thankfully I was being careful and had the gun aimed where it would do the least amount of damage. The least amount of damage is still a lot.

You get a good idea of the power of a 12 gauge loaded with buckshot by blowing a hole in a solid wood door. You also realize just how much smoke and other airborne material is produced, because the blast will cause a smoke detector to start screeching. The door didn't look too bad from the shotgun side, but the other side was a different story. Large chunks of wood hung from the curtains covering the window opposite the door. The solid red Hudson Bay blanket looked like a porcupine. For months, small splinters were picked out of the clothes that were in the pile of recently washed laundry thrown on a chair next to the bed.

My 21st birthday was memorable as well. This milestone was reached when the drinking age was still 18 in some states, but 21 was still a big deal. I was working at the strip club, and they had a tradition of bringing in a guy dressed as an ape when the birthday girl was on stage and topless. That must have been a job that the guys at the balloon store fought over.

Another particularly interesting birthday was my 28th. I was working for a firearms manufacturer north of Atlanta. One of the women I worked with came to the celebration with her boyfriend. We started at a Cajun restaurant where we drank quite a bit. After leaving the restaurant, we stopped at a convenience store.

Animal, who was a big drinker, sauntered into the store with his Desert Eagle strapped in his concealed carry holster. If it had stayed concealed, there wouldn't have been an issue. However, Animal was wasted, and his vest was hanging open, making this an open carry situation at a 7-11 after dark. The clerk at the convenience store wasn't feeling good about the armed, drunk biker and a call went out to the police. They were surprisingly mellow about the whole firearms situation and just wanted us to leave. We simply moved the gathering across the street to discuss where we'd go next.

What followed was an interesting conversation where my coworker announced that she'd been breast fed on scotch. When you're hanging out with a bunch of drunken bikers (or sober bikers for that matter), there was only one response you could expect, and Animal spoke right up: "I sure would like to suck on those titties." I don't know what Jane thought she'd receive for feedback on her comment. It's entirely possible that she wasn't accustomed to hanging out with bikers and was usually the wildest person present. Apparently she didn't expect what I felt was the most obvious response to her proclamation, and the night went downhill quickly.

Jane wanted Animal to apologize, and he wouldn't. I don't blame him. Then she wanted her boyfriend to beat up Animal. This was absurd. He was about a foot shorter and was one of those guys who wears polo shirts and white sneakers; not the kind of guy that goes around picking fights with drunken bikers. That could have ended there, except now Jane refused to go anywhere with her boyfriend, nor would she get in the vehicle that Animal was riding in. This required some quick creative ride-sharing decisions, and she got in the Bronco II with Buck and me.

The next stop was the liquor store, as though we really needed more booze. Something was said that clued Jane into the fact that everyone, including her boyfriend, Animal and herself, were going back to our place. She jumped out of the vehicle saying that she was going to hitchhike home - over fifty miles away. I jumped out after her and tried to grab her to get her back in the car. She fell on the ground while weaseling out of her coat, which I was holding onto. Next thing I know, she's kicking me with her spike heels. I was trying to get her off the ground, but I got pulled off by Buck who assumed I was jumping in for the fight. Jane finally got up and stomped off into the night, eventually getting a ride all the way home from a cop who picked her up on the side of the road.

5

A couple of months after my 22nd birthday I wasn't feeling well and went to the doctor. The friend that took me kept saying I was pregnant, which never occurred to me. I was. There could not have been a worse time. An outline of the scenario:

- Buck was doing better than right after his mother died, but he was still extremely paranoid

- We were both unemployed: no money and no health insurance.

- We were living way back in the country, in a 200 square foot shed, far from any source of employment.

- We didn't have electricity or running water, and that wasn't going to change soon.

- The old Panhead was our only source of transportation.

In addition to the above, I was also an alcoholic but didn't recognize it at the time. I wasn't one of those drunks that downed a case of beer a day, but when I did drink, I didn't stop. I wouldn't go too far out of the way to get booze, but if it was available, I was all over it. I also liked to smoke weed. By that time, other recreational drugs were mostly out of the picture, but if cocaine was available, I'd do it.

But there it was. Buck was happy about it. I was terrified. He said he'd get a job. I hauled water uphill from the spring, heated it up on the Coleman stove, and did my best to pretend that everything was going to be OK. Buck got a job working with a friend of ours, erecting forms for concrete walls. Brutal. It was hard work, and it was nasty. Buck would come home caked with red clay, and there was no way to wash clothes. He didn't go to work often, which meant no money for things like food or doctor bills.

I had a chrome transmission that was worth a good chunk of cash. In fact its value was close to what the doctor was requesting by a certain date to guarantee that he'd show up for the birth of our child. Tim, our friend in northwest Georgia, had the money and was willing to buy it, so Buck took a trip over there to make the sale. He came back with a pound of pot. When I expressed my concern, I got slapped. The situation was hopeless.

Toward the end of my pregnancy, Buck had started working at a job in Atlanta and was living, partying, and sleeping around the greater metro area during the week. I was going to school at the junior college about two miles from the property, thanks to my parents' commitment to my education.

For a while, I was able to drive to school in a pickup truck. The only problem was that the shift linkage was broken, and in order to put the truck into drive, I had to open the hood, shift the truck into gear, and jump in the truck while it was driving away. That was the better scenario. Before long, the truck died altogether and I was walking to school. The route was down one side of a mountain and up the other to school, making it the proverbial "uphill both ways."

I never thought I would have been happy to own a mobile home, but I was thrilled when we were able to purchase one. With the home came a kitchen stove that would run on LP gas. We got a big propane tank and hooked the gas up to the range so I could simply light the burners with a match. That made it a lot easier to heat water. Even though we didn't have running water coming in or a septic tank on the drainage side, I could wash the dishes in the sink using water heated on the stovetop, and the water would empty into a drum under the house. The bathroom was still an outhouse – or the far side of a clump of trees.

We were now able to heat our home easier in winter with an old propane heater. I shudder when I think about the time I arrived home to find the heater hadn't been turned down before we left and flames were leaping out of the top. It's a miracle the trailer didn't burn. We still hauled water and lit the house at night with a Coleman lantern and flashlights. Another miracle – we didn't die from carbon monoxide poisoning.

I had an especially exciting time dealing with some loaner pets. One of Buck's brothers, Jerry D, had some pit bulls he'd raised to be vicious guard dogs. They were tethered to their houses with huge logging chains, which made them not only mean but also really strong. Jerry D could no longer keep his dogs where he was living, and apparently the clubhouse wasn't an option. One of the clubhouses I'd visited with Buck had an interesting setup: a sizable piece of property with a high fence all the way around. Inside the fence, you stayed on the well-lit, visible paths or you were dog food. That would have been an appropriate home. But no, we became the caregivers for these chunks of evil muscle at our home.

Early on, one of the dogs got loose and attacked Buck. Buck was no lightweight, but it was a battle to keep the dog from killing him. Buck managed to wrestle the dog down and got it hooked back up. If it was just about anyone else who'd been attacked, there's no question the person would have been dead or mangled for life.

I had a red Doberman, which we kept on a chain because he wanted to play with the pit bulls. It was more of a taunting, and I knew that if one of the dogs ever got a hold of him, he was dead. I was resigned to the situation. I hated it, but I didn't have a say.

One day one of my classmates gave me a ride home. She dropped me off by the trailer door. After I got inside I realized the male pit bull was loose. That's when things got tense. It was still a few days before Buck would be back home, and I was going to have to leave the trailer at some point -- not just to go to school the next day, but also for a trip to the outhouse. I was becoming very upset about the situation, and the baby was turning somersaults inside of me. While trying to figure out what to do, I saw the black monster go over to my Doberman on the chain and latch on to his throat.

I'd had enough of being held prisoner by the fucking dog and grabbed the shotgun. Buck kept the Mossberg 12 gauge loaded with alternating buck shot and slugs. I've always been pretty good with a shotgun. The dog was in trouble. Because I didn't want to shoot my own dog, the first shot was aimed at the pit bull's ass. Buck shot from a 12 gauge was enough to get him to let go of my dog. The slug through his head ended the situation. Great. I'd just killed one of the brothers' dogs. Six months pregnant, no hope of electricity or running water in the near future, a dangerous madman for a partner and father of my child, and now I'd shot and killed a one percenter's dog. Life was interesting.

I was ready to shoot my own dog before too long. All he'd do was bark at the carcass laid out next to him. I was practically sick to my stomach by them, but at least I could go outside to puke without fear of being ripped apart. Surprisingly, Buck wasn't too angry with me for shooting the dog. One day when Buck was back in the city working for the week, I heard a motorcycle coming up the road. As it got closer, I saw it was Jerry D. Uh-oh.

"I heard you shot my dog."

"Yeah, sorry."

"I wanted you to know it's OK."

"Thanks."

Then he got on his bike and left.

We had a no-frills birth plan, if you could even call it a plan. I opted for natural childbirth, not for any higher purpose but because it was cheaper. Our theory was that women had been doing this for years, so no big deal. No classes, no preparation, no nothing. In fact, the only transportation we had was the Panhead, and I was prepared to jump on the back and ride the hour to the hospital when labor started. My mother was supposed to be visiting with a rental car when the baby was due, so she could get us home. Fortunately, someone gave us a van about two weeks before the baby was born. Once I went into labor, I realized that making the hour trip to the hospital on the p-pad, on the back of a rigid frame, would have consisted of me screaming for him to pull over every two minutes while I went through contractions.

I managed to pull off natural childbirth while cussing the midwife and yelling at everyone attending to "get the fucking thing out of me." It was a long ten hours of contractions that started two minutes apart at around eight that morning. When I asked for Demerol a couple of hours into the adventure, I was told he'd be out any minute, hence my hostility toward everyone involved.

At 6:36 that evening, my son was born. Aside from some jaundice, he was a healthy baby boy. I think I was more terrified than anything. I had no idea how I was going to care for a baby when my own survival was questionable. I had no idea how to care for a baby if he'd been born into perfect circumstances.

I'd never had the desire to be a mother, but after Dan was born, I couldn't imagine life without him. Keeping him alive was the only thing that mattered to me. I was still drinking and smoking pot, but I never considered that to be a problem. The problem was the crazy, dangerous guy who lived with us.

6

It was hard to tell what would send Buck into the depths of Hell or how long he'd stay there. It was common in the best of times to be forced to sit for hours and listen to Buck rant about how the company he worked for was trying to screw him and the rest of the workers. Any attempt to explain a possible alternate point of view would make me the enemy.

Dan was nine months old to the day when Buck and I got married very unceremoniously at the court house. Dan was about two and a half years old when we got electricity. My parents loaned us money to dig a well, and I borrowed more money to dig a septic tank. I graduated with an Associate's degree and went to work in Atlanta.

I would rush home from work every day, stopping briefly to pick Dan up at day care. I often debated whether I should pick something up to cook for dinner or if that would make me late enough to be accused of having an affair. I'd race back home as quickly as I could and then be filled with dread as I pulled in the driveway. I never knew what to expect. But I hung in there, hoping that Buck would return to normal.

We'd been barely scraping by, but we were both working when 1990 rolled around. Because we were just getting back on our feet, we declined when some friends invited us to a Superbowl party and chili cook-off. I could make chili, but we had one piece of meat in the freezer for the next week or two, and I wanted to save it. Besides, we couldn't afford to buy beer, and who wants to go to a Superbowl party without beer? Our friends insisted, saying that they'd have plenty of beer and it would be a great time. We relented, and I made a pot of chili with my lone slab of beef.

We went to the party. The hosts were offering everyone beer... except us. They were passing joints... as long as we weren't in the circle. At first it seemed like a simple oversight, but it became obvious after an hour of the slights that we were being excluded. I grabbed my crock pot of chili, and we left.

When we were in our worst of times, with no money or utilities, there was a lot of bumming going on. Smoking a joint was a tranquilizer for Buck's tortured mind, and he had no problem showing up at someone's house and asking to get high. Because he was so intimidating, nobody declined his requests. Showers, laundry, food, alcohol and pot: it was all up for grabs. I was uncomfortable with the implied begging, but Buck was fine with it. I think it was left over from his days in the club; people should be happy that he graced them with his presence. His first wife, Suzie, had no problem playing the entitlement game. It made me uneasy. I felt that this particular group of "friends" at the Superbowl party had grown a collectively huge set of balls, and they were trying to get payback. We left the party.

I was hurt. We'd all had good times and bad. We had contributed at times, in various ways. Our kids were the same ages and were friends. I was angry and devastated. Buck took it to a level beyond my comprehension. He was convinced that the group of friends, who were all related either by blood or marriage, were trying to kill us and steal our property. Yes we had a nice parcel, but it wasn't the kind or value of property people killed over. Buck started producing examples of what they'd done to hurt us, all of which were outlandish. He started gathering weapons to go over and kill the lot of them. I finally had the idea to suggest that if he killed them, we'd have to raise their children. That put an end to the ambush, but Buck's fragile mind had cracked.

He didn't come back quickly. In fact, the paranoia grew rampantly. I was trying to keep life at an even keel, but I had no idea what was brewing. I was working for a firearms manufacturer and he was working for an engineering firm in the same town. Even though our work schedules were much different, he insisted we ride into town together. He'd get off earlier than I did, and when I'd leave the building, he was waiting out front. One day when I came out, he wasn't in the pickup. I was surprised to see him exit the building after me and asked what he'd been doing. He said he'd gone to talk to Bob, the national sales manager, about working for the company. When I got home, the manager's secretary Jane (the crazy drunk woman from my 28th birthday story), called and asked if everything was OK. It seemed strange, but all was fine.

After I arrived at work the following day, I was called down to the conference room. Cops everywhere. What Buck had done the previous day was to go into Bob's office and tell him that Jane had drugged me, and I'd been raped by six guys at work. I was mortified. Strangely, I was more embarrassed about what they thought of me being with this guy than terrified about his state of mind. I must have gotten to the point where nothing he thought surprised me. They needed to verify whether it was true or not, and then they offered help. To this day I want to kick myself for not accepting their assistance. That was probably the one opportunity I had to get out of there without losing everything I owned. But I didn't want their help.

By the end of the day, I'd made some calls and was trying to figure out how to get him into a psychiatric facility. I was afraid. He was always fully armed, and an armed, paranoid man with a history of violence comes under the category of "worst nightmare." Fortunately I wasn't totally alone. Someone from work had called to have a local police officer there when Buck was expected in the afternoon. Also, we had been attending church, and I'd called our minister to help convince Buck to check himself into the hospital down the street.

When Buck arrived at the building, Father Bob and I met him outside. Buck was extremely agitated and said that he couldn't go back to work anymore. He'd "popped" one of the employees. He proceeded to tell our minister that I was the one with the problem, that "...all anyone has to do is say the word and she'll drop to her knees." So if I hadn't been totally mortified that morning when I'd learned of his accusation, imagine how I felt when he told our preacher I was giving random blow jobs to any guy who came up with the magic word. Guys, I know what you're thinking. There is no magic word.

Father Bob had a better grip on how to handle the situation. I couldn't understand why he was accepting Buck's accusations. Of course there was no arguing with Buck, but when your husband makes that proclamation to anyone who'll listen, the tendency is to deny it. We convinced Buck that he should go to the hospital, because the cops would soon be there to take him to jail for the assault on his coworker. Eventually Father Bob got in the truck with Buck and the handgun hanging from the rifle rack, and off they went to the hospital. I followed in Bob's car.

We later learned that Buck accused his co-worker of raping me. I've never met the man. I don't even remember his name. I'm sure he remembers us though, because Buck's idea of "popping" him in the face hospitalized him. We got Buck checked into the hospital, but the Sheriff's Department would be waiting for his release. The hospital jacked Buck up with Thorazine, which he hated and refused to take. After a week they decided there was nothing else they could do for him and called me to come pick him up. Excuse me? They announced his release two days after a family session with the doctor. I'd told Buck that one of the men from the church had gone to the trailer and removed every weapon inside. What I didn't tell him was that the guy was appalled by the amount of guns, knives, and assorted other lethal weapons he'd found. Buck went berserk, screaming that he'd never be able to defend us against the demons and all the people who were trying to kill us. And yes, the hospital saw fit to release him. It had something to do with insurance. Or maybe they were afraid of him too.

As soon as Buck was released, he was arrested for assaulting his co-worker. Former coworker. He was bailed out quickly, and by that time he had managed to get his emotions under control. While he appeared calm on the surface, the psychosis was simmering.

Toward the end of June, I mentioned to Buck that a friend wanted me to babysit for her kids the next day. For some reason, this particular statement was offensive, but when you're dealing with someone for whom logic is not a reality, there usually is no reason. Not that makes sense in my world.

I remember the flowered wallpaper in the budget mobile home's bathroom. I remember the large mirror mounted on the wall. I remember the small shelves I'd covered with contact paper and hung over the vanity. I remember the 9mm pistol loaded with 19 rounds of hollow point ammunition, and one in the chamber, pointed at my head. There was always one in the chamber.

"You have a problem. Your parents hypnotized you when you were young, and they pimped you out."

"What are you talking about? My parents would never do anything like that."

"They did, and you don't remember because you were hypnotized."

"Well how do you know about it?"

Wrong question, because again, logic had no place in his world. I started thinking about the man at our church whose brother had recently committed a murder-suicide, killing his wife and children and then himself. Suddenly I understood how this shit happens. Suddenly I understood that of course mothers who drown their children are insane. Normal people don't do that. I wasn't only worried about my life, but would happen to my son sleeping in the bedroom that shared a wall with the bathroom.

He continued to make these crazy accusations for what seemed like hours. Maybe it wasn't. Maybe it's that time stands still when you're sure you're about to die. I kept trying to explain the flaws in his thinking, which only proved to him that what he said was true. In a flash of brilliance, I told him he was right, and I needed help. As quickly as the storm started, it was over.

Despite the fact that Buck was in his own world, by the time daylight rolled around, he knew he'd screwed up. He'd lightened up quite a bit, and when I left with my son to go babysit for my friend, I suggested he go to Tim's house for a couple of days to give me some time alone. To my surprise, he agreed without suggesting that I wanted him to leave so I could screw some poor bastard who was dumb enough to get involved.

Marjorie, my friend in New York who'd been there when Buck went on his demon burning spree, had offered me and Dan a place to stay until I get on my feet. As I watched the kids play, I wondered if it was possible to leave behind everything I owned, including many family heirloom antiques (an act that wouldn't be forgiven for years), and start a new life a thousand miles away as a single mom.

While babysitting, Buck showed up with the deed to his property, signed over to me. Although we were concerned that the guy he'd hospitalized a month earlier would attempt to sue Buck, I knew the signed deed was a peace offering for his behavior the night before. A dozen roses would be cheaper and just as effective – a thought I kept to myself.

With Buck at Tim's for a couple of days, which was over an hour away, my son and I went into town to pick up some things we needed for the trip – and the rest of our lives. Coming around the end of an aisle at the K-Mart, I spotted Buck at the gun counter dressed completely in woodland camo and buying bullets. I grabbed my son and headed toward the opposite end of the store, keeping an eye on the front so I could watch him leave. Although we weren't ready to make our escape, we couldn't go home. Dan and I got in the car and disappeared.

7

Dan and I headed to New York. I was excited, terrified, relieved and numb. Although we'd left almost everything behind, I had bills to pay and no job. I had a child who would probably never see his father again. I had a couple of guns in a state that doesn't take kindly to firearm possession. We were alive.

Marjorie had left Tim to move in with Artie. Artie lived with his mother in a huge mansion in New York that had been in the family for years. Artie's mom had the bottom floor, and Artie and Marjorie lived on the second floor, which was a home in itself with a couple of bathrooms, four bedrooms, a kitchen and living room. The second floor was larger than most places I've lived in my adult life.

Artie was a friend of mine before I'd met Marjorie and before he and Marjorie had met. He used to come visit Jimmy and me and buy up old Harleys that had been stashed in barns and hadn't seen the light of day for decades. Artie and I laugh a lot when we talk about stories from the past, but even though we had some crazy fun times, back then he usually irritated me. He had money, but he always wanted a deal. We were always struggling to keep a roof over our heads, and it never appeared that he respected that.

A year earlier, Marjorie had called and told me she'd moved in with Artie. I offered a half-hearted "Congratulations". It was more like, "Really? Is that good?" But I softened quite a bit when Artie went along with Marjorie's suggestion that I stay with them. In fact, it became clear before too long that Marjorie had some serious issues while Artie truly was a good friend.

The first couple of years were pretty rough. Marjorie's benevolence was short-lived. Her offer to have us stay as long as we needed to was more like an offer to stay until she tired of having a small child in the house. I was hoping to save up a couple of months pay before moving out, but it was clear that wasn't soon enough. Marjorie wavered between making me feel like a valued friend and treating me like a charity project.

One day Marjorie told me that a mutual friend of ours from Georgia was coming to visit. On the day he was due to arrive, I asked Marjorie what time I should be there for dinner. Her response?

"A jeweler friend of ours from Atlanta will be here. It's just going to be the three of us."

It was Jimmy and I who introduced Marjorie

to that jeweler friend of hers. And while she sat there with her nose in the air, I thought of the times that I'd gotten high with her jeweler friend and sat in jail with her jeweler friend and all the time behind bars her jeweler friend did for kidnapping. Marjorie was big on appearances, just what I'd left behind years before. One would have thought that would be the end of that friendship, but I was still grateful that she'd given us a way out of our nightmare and felt I owed her something.

Life went on. I took my first job in New York as an MIS Manager for a conference center. In the early nineties, that meant maintaining PCs on a local area network (LAN) along with a Unix mini-computer that ran the property management system. With that job came telecommunications responsibilities. It's a logical relationship now, but that was before the Internet. The phone room held a monstrous PBX switch that looked like the early super computers. It was massive and intimidating. To make changes on telephone sets, I had to dial in on a 1200 baud modem and enter commands that were memorized or found in a manual. Color monitors and graphical user interfaces, like Windows, existed but weren't prevalent. The main distribution panel (phone wires going everywhere in the building) for the conference center covered a 30 foot wall. I learned to use the tools of the phone guy's trade. It wasn't long before I preferred telephony over PCs and LANs.

I struggled to pay the rent and over $200 a week for childcare. I was constantly terrified that Buck would somehow find us. I made new friends and continued to put up with Marjorie's condescending ways. At one point I went to Dan's school and spoke to the guidance counselor about our situation. I wanted to be proactive in case Dan had issues in school. I was also worried that Buck's psychiatric disorder might be genetic. The counselor asked me if I'd been drinking a lot more, as if I was the one with the problem. I quickly told her that alcohol was not an issue for me.

That weekend, Dan and I went with Marjorie to a church holiday dinner in upstate New York. I had a couple of glasses of wine and a shot of some crazy Greek liquor, Ouzo. Marjorie was right there, drink for drink, and she suddenly decided it was time to go. I felt fine, but when we hit the roadblock and I admitted to having a glass of wine with dinner, the state troopers decided to do a breathalyzer test and I ended up with a DWAI. Now I was forced to look at how much of my screwed up life was my fault.

I immediately quit drinking and started going to meetings. I had friends who couldn't understand why I quit, because we all knew people who were a lot worse off than me. Then there was Marjorie, who was happy to support my recovery one moment, while in the next breath telling me about great parties I'd missed with lots of alcohol and drugs. Someone new in AA will very stubbornly let old friends go when told they need to stay away from the people, places and things that are associated with drinking. I was no different. How could I turn my back on the woman who'd done so much for me? It takes some time without booze to see how damaging these sick relationships really are.

I started going to church, because even though I wasn't convinced there was a God, my life always seemed to get easier when I was going. This time was no exception as the church helped me pay for childcare and a couple of the expenses associated with my arrest.

I was sober for a few months and eventually started drinking again. After all, Marjorie was the only person who would tell me I had a problem. People in the rooms of AA will tell you that you start up where you left off. It seemed like any crazy drunk thing that I hadn't yet done, I did over the next year. I spent the year drinking, drinking more, doing things I'd regret, and drinking to get over it. At a summer employee party at the conference center, I filled a "Super Soaker" water gun with tequila and shot it at people. I'm sure I drove while drinking again, and likely with my child in the car. I slept with a friend's boyfriend. There were probably other things I did, but the point is, I was worse off in a matter of weeks than I'd been before I quit drinking.

On my thirtieth birthday, all of my friends showed up with bottles of tequila. Over the next couple of months, I'd settle down at night with a drink or two or three. I ran out of tequila about the time that Artie lost his leg in a motorcycle accident.

I wasn't with Artie the night of the accident, but there were rumors, and the rumors were believable. I've never asked, because it seems that asking Artie if he was drunk that night would be judgmental, and I don't feel that the pain he suffered was deserved in any way. Besides, it didn't matter if he was drunk or not. I was faced with the reality that my drinking could be devastating to my son, either by hurting him or hurting myself to where I couldn't care for him. I started going back to meetings, although I was still having a drink here and there, not quite ready to give it up for good.

A group of us went to Americade, a big touring motorcycle rally in Lake George, New York, to set up Artie's booth and sell his biker camping gear while he was in the hospital. The highlight for me was when Teddy let me ride his Shovelhead. It had been a long time since I'd ridden, but it came back quickly.

One of the women in our group was someone new to me. She had been sober for a while. She gently helped me realize that I needed to stop altogether. It was impossible for me to have any fun anymore while drinking, since I knew it was a bad idea. I had my last drink on June 13, 1992. By the Grace of God, that date will remain the date of my last drink forever.

Speaking of God… I know that the mention of God and a higher power are what kept my father from getting anything out of the Alcoholics Anonymous program. It wasn't so much that he didn't believe as much as he hated religion. His mother's beliefs kept her from getting the medical care she needed. He wasn't about to hang out with anyone that mentioned God or a higher power. I wasn't a believer myself, but I wasn't going to let that stand in my way. I'd do what I had to, include make up some version of a higher power that worked for me. I saw what my father's life had become, and I knew that my life could be much better. I wasn't going to let semantics get in the way. Alcoholism eventually killed my father.

Through the church, I got a job at a community health center in early sobriety. My office was shoved into a closet in between the Vice President's office and the HIV counseling office. Many of the patients in the counseling office were recovering addicts. Because of our proximity, I became friends with a few of the HIV patients. This was in the early nineties, and HIV always led to AIDS and death. When I needed someone to speak to during my work day, I could turn to Dennis, who had become a counselor for addicts living with HIV and AIDS at an outreach program down a block or two from the health center. While I knew that my problems were nothing compared to what he was facing, Dennis never failed to listen, be compassionate, and help me through my troubles. When I'd mention that I felt petty being upset about things like work relationships and paying the rent while he was facing death, he was quick to point out that we weren't there to compare our problems.

When I was hired as the Operations Manager at the health center, I asked for the telephony responsibilities as well. I left the health center for a pure telephone job, installing and repairing PBX switches for a small business owned by a former Bell employee. I had jobs that ranged from a mob-run produce distributor in the Bronx (where the Vice President tried to fondle me in the phone room) to an installation at Kykuit, the Rockefeller estate in Tarrytown, NY.

I loved working at Kykuit. I had to replace all the telephone sets in the rooms of the estate as well as a complete new installation in what is now known as the Pocantico Center. I worked in rooms on the tour as well as those off-limits to most everyone. One day in a small closet in the basement, I found a door jamb that had been used to record the heights of the children as they grew: Nelson and David and their brothers were all there. It struck me as an intimate peek into a very public and prominent family. When my boss refused to pay a second worker to help me get the phones going on a weekend before the visit of the leader of a European country, I enlisted my ten-year-old son to help me locate the original wiring and connect it to the new.

Throughout these years, staying sober got easier, and life got better. Dan was growing up, and I didn't have to pay for childcare any longer. I'd set his alarm and then leave for work before he'd wake and get ready for school. He was eight years old when we started doing that. Ice hockey started around that time too, the cost of which far eclipsed childcare. I couldn't afford it, but I made it work. I was the only single mom on Dan's hockey team and was one of the few who worked outside of the home. There were no Harley riders in this group. I still had my biker friends, but I saw them less and less. I yearned to ride again, but barely being able to pay the rent made the dream of owning my own motorcycle seem impossible.

I was still afraid that Buck would find me, and I often had nightmares that I was back on the property with no hope of leaving. I was trapped. If I saw a big guy with suspenders and a beard, my heart would skip a beat and I'd hide until I could be sure it wasn't him.

After I'd left, Buck continued to live in the trailer on the property and drive the truck we both owned. Over time I paid off the Bronco II we'd left Georgia in as well as a couple of other debts, but Buck paid for nothing. The Ranger he was driving got repossessed. Then the trailer was taken. The two items together cost him $400 per month. Even by early nineties standard, it wasn't much. Buck could have sold the antique roll top desk and paid the mobile home off, but instead the trailer got repossessed with everything inside. The kicker was that the finance company was coming after me for the outstanding balance, which made me wonder where those antiques ended up. I had no sympathy for Buck or the fact that he'd signed the property over to me. I was too angry for sympathy. I'd been forced to abandon our home, leaving everything but my child behind, and now I had to pay for everything I lost as well.

I contacted a real estate agent in Georgia and put the property up for sale. It took a couple of years, but about the time I was contemplating returning to college full time, it sold. I had considered going to school in the evenings, but it would take forever, and I would completely miss Dan's life from age 10 until whenever. I wasn't willing to do that. Selling the property made it easier to attend an engineering college in northern New York State. I had a lot to pay off that was related to the property and debts incurred with Buck.

I was a better mother during those years. Because I was in school only a few hours a day, I was able to participate more in Dan's classroom activities. I could chaperone field trips and attend classroom parties. I even coached an Odyssey of the Mind team. I was out of my league on that endeavor, but the kids had fun. I still wanted a motorcycle, but it was unrealistic since I needed to save as much money as I could to get through school.

I got involved in my own extra-curricular activities. After freezing in the stands for a few years, I wanted to play ice hockey. I managed to get a women's club team going at school. I worked the subject of women's hockey into every project I had to complete for my Technical Communications degree. I made presentations, negotiated ice time, and did my best to work with the school's athletic director who was notoriously against women's hockey. I had nothing but the best intentions for the team, but apparently I was lacking in something, because when my friend Dennis passed away from AIDS and I left school to go to the funeral, I arrived back to find that I'd been relieved of my duties with the hockey team. After all of my successes at Clarkson, and there were many, this cowardly way of taking me down still taints my memories of the school. Fortunately life goes on after college, and I had other things to do.

Before I was out of school, I'd landed a job at the phone company in New York as an Outside Plant Engineer. I was in Heaven until my first day on the job. I quickly realized what a bunch of schmucks I was working with. It amazed me that a person who considered himself more intelligent than the blue collar union employees could be such a foul-mouthed, loud, pig. Even worse was that nobody made an effort to tell him to shut up. Everyone in the group went along with his constant offensive squawking, and when I spoke up and asked him to save his comments on his sexual escapades for lunch with the boys, I was immediately ostracized by the whole group.

It was a particularly rough time emotionally. My father died two weeks before I graduated. I'm extremely thankful that we had a decent relationship before he went. I knew he was miserable in life, and we never saw each other, but I would call him when Dan did especially well in a hockey game or to discuss a major sporting event, and I found myself missing him more than I anticipated.

A couple of months after that, I was diagnosed with cancer. This is particularly scary when you are a single parent with no close relatives. However, there was a bright side. I finally kicked Marjorie out of my life. I was looking at a hysterectomy to treat the cancer at the beginning of the new year, and she was insisting I go to a New Year's party at her sister's. I tried to explain that it wasn't a good time for me. I was worried about Dan more than anything, and how he was going to live while I was in the hospital. The doctors wouldn't know if the cancer had spread until they did the procedure. Going to a party where everyone would be drinking was the last thing I wanted to do. I don't know what her agenda was, but she was not going to let me off the hook. It appalled me that I was dealing with this disease and all she could think about was what mattered to her. I haven't spoken to her since.

Everything went well with the operation. I had to stay out of work for 6 weeks, which didn't break my heart. It was scary financially, but we managed. Going back to work, nobody asked how I was or gave any indication that they cared if I lived or died.

I became virtually useless in my position, since nobody would work with me and only one of my projects was funded. I begged to be allowed to transfer to a different department, but there was a policy against transferring before you were in a position for two years. I counted down the days and applied for an installation and repair supervisor's job in New Hampshire. My boss in engineering had the nerve to tell me that the repair garage I was going to had a bad reputation. Like anything could have been worse than the last two years of my professional life.

Moving to New Hampshire brought higher pay and a lower cost of living. The company helped me purchase a log cabin on a lake, which was my dream home. It was small and had a steep, deep rut-filled driveway, but it was perfect for me. Because Dan was incredibly smart and I was still on the low end of income (compared to most families), he got a scholarship for a boarding school. Public school had ceased being any challenge at all, and I was afraid that his boredom would turn my good kid into trouble.

A little more freedom ensued. In addition to knowing my son was getting the best education possible, I could date. It was the beginning of the Internet dating era, and I gave it a try. Searching with Harley-Davidson as a keyword gave me a few options, and I tried them out. One guy I met in Massachusetts. He was a typical old Harley rider who was working on the Big Dig in Boston. He took me for a ride, and I thought I was going to die. It wasn't my first ride with a Harley owner since I'd left Buck, and I was beginning to appreciate both Buck's and Jimmy's riding skills. Both of my exes rode rigid frame Panheads with suicide clutches, which are far more difficult to operate, and I never worried about my safety. This guy was an idiot, and I had to tell him to take me back to my car. That was it.

Another date that came up in my search for a biker consisted of wake boarding on Lake Sunapee. The guy had a boat and a Harley and his own home and all kinds of toys. I had the feeling he was pretty straight-laced, and seeing as how we were going out on a boat and I'd be in a bathing suit, I warned him about my tattoos. They were far less acceptable in the general population at the time. The morning before I was going on the date, I somehow managed to press my arm into the end of a hot hair dryer, leaving a suspiciously Wicca-looking burn mark. Not only was I tattooed, but I was branded. Lovely. After getting off the water, where I did an amazing job at wake-boarding, we went back to his house. He showed me his Harley - that thing stuffed back behind a bunch of other toys. The guy was a Harley owner, but he was not a Harley rider.

I was struggling with analyzing what I was looking for in a relationship. I wanted a real biker, but every real biker I'd ever known was a drinker. I couldn't have that. I had no idea where I was going to fit in. A pivotal moment in my life occurred while waiting for a prescription to be filled at the pharmacy in Lebanon. I picked up a motorcycle magazine, saw a review on the new Harley-Davidsons and realized that I was finally in the position to buy my own motorcycle.

8

Going to a dealership and buying a Harley-Davidson was not as simple as I thought it would be. Those were the days when most dealers tacked on as much as $3,000 to the manufacturer's suggested retail price of a new Harley. On top of that, you were lucky if you got something close to what you wanted after waiting six months to a year to get it. There was nothing on the showroom floors, except maybe a few Sportsters. I wanted to ride, but I wasn't going to settle for anything less than a big twin.

After looking at all the options, I decided to buy a 2001 Softail Standard. In the past I've always ridden rigid frames, and the Softail would give me the same seating position but with a suspension. I wanted forward controls and a wide glide front end, but I didn't want all the extras that come on the more expensive Softails. I knew I'd want to customize it myself, and I didn't want to pay extra for chrome parts that I'd be removing. I didn't want fuel injection and stuck with the carburetor. The parts guy at the dealership talked me into a 42mm Mikuni, and in hindsight, I wish I'd kept the CV carb. There were three color options: red, blue and black. Again, I knew this would change, so I chose black as the best temporary color. After that, all I could do was wait.

While the bike was on order, I met a guy through an online dating site. He wasn't a biker, but we got along well. Our first date was night skiing. It was pretty cool. As we were riding up the chairlift, the full moon was rising above the mountain behind us. Not too long into the night, my date took a good fall, what's known as a "yard sale." There was stuff everywhere. He'd been on the edge of the trail, and one of his skis disappeared. It was gone, with the only hope being that sometime in the spring, the stray board would appear. It was an old ski, and Darren was a good sport. He got down the slope on one ski and we called it a night.

Darren and I got serious. He was the first non-biker I'd been seriously involved with. His parents lived in an affluent coastal Maine resort town and were wealthy. The clothing, the dinners, the educations, and the conversations... everything reminded me of how I'd been raised. There was some comfort in that, although I'd very consciously left that world behind. Having been through such hard times, I started thinking that it would be nice to be back in an atmosphere of LL Bean and social grace.

After very impatiently waiting six months for my motorcycle to arrive, I received a call from the dealership telling me that my bike was in. Very exciting! Within minutes I received a call from Buck's niece telling me that he was dead. He'd been found in a storage unit in Chattanooga, and the service was going to be in Knoxville.

I asked Dan if he wanted to go to Knoxville for the funeral, and he did. It was still scary for me to think about going there, but I had to trust that he really was dead. Certainly he wouldn't have made this up, right?

This all happened at the beginning of Laconia Race and Rally Week. I'd harassed my dealer continually about getting my bike, and with it being the busiest week of the year, they didn't want to spend time on dealer prep. This really bugged me, but with Buck's death and subsequent funeral, I wasn't in such a hurry anymore. They were glad that I was off their backs for a week.

I told my son a few times over the years that once he was old enough to take care of himself, I would try to find Buck and arrange a visit if he wanted. Dan had his own nightmares from his early years, and he always denied any interest in going. Now he didn't have a choice. His father was dead. I felt bad about my feelings, but I was relieved. I knew that his actions were a result of his tortured mind, but I didn't have to worry about him showing up some day and killing me or kidnapping Dan. The nightmares stopped overnight. We made plans to go to Knoxville for the funeral.

When Dan and I were checking in to the hotel in Knoxville, I picked up a brochure from a rack: *Knoxville. Who knew?* We looked at each other and laughed at the irony. We'd left Georgia eleven years before, almost to the day. We'd moved several times, from the suburbs of New York City to the Canadian border, back to southern New York and then to New Hampshire. Who knew where we'd be at any point in time? Who knew what would lead us there? Neither of us had to say a word. We knew.

Dan and I went to the funeral in our rented car. The only brother there was Crazy Dave, who'd been a close friend before he was in the club. In fact, he was one of the first people I'd met when I moved to Georgia from Florida, and I'd known him long before I met Buck. There he was, now the president of the Atlanta chapter and traveling with a bodyguard, I assumed, from a support club. It was the first time I'd seen anyone from my Georgia past in the eleven years since we left, and I was glad it was Crazy.

After the funeral, everyone went to Buck's sister's house. The same sister who had said many years before that she didn't know why I put up with Buck had completely changed her tune when I had called her after Dan and I escaped. Maybe I'd violated "in sickness and in health," but there was no vow that said I was required to sacrifice my son and die at my husband's hands. Nonetheless, she was openly gloating when I entered the house and saw a lot of my valuable artwork on the walls of her double-wide.

I don't understand why people get so greedy in the middle of grief. As the anger washed over me, I had to remind myself that I'd let go of that stuff, that my life was much better now, and that I was free. She allowed Dan and his half-brother to go through a small box of Buck's things and take what they wanted. Dan grabbed a few knives, including one that I'd given to Buck and another that was mine, at my quiet request.

I asked to see his motorcycle and went out to the garage. It was torn apart, and there were more boxes of my belongings there. I took the license plate off the Panhead basket case as a keepsake for Dan. I scanned the boxes on the shelves and saw my nativity set that I missed every Christmas. It was a small trinket that cost less than $10, but I loved it. The carved wooden nativity participants fit inside the closed doors of the barn for storage when the season was over. Baby Jesus was missing, but I could come up with a replacement.

I refused to simply take items. I'd left him and I'd left them. Regardless of what made sense or what the law was, I treated it all as though everything now belonged to Buck's sister, and told her I wanted the license plate and the nativity set. Fortunately she offered no resistance. Dan and I headed back to New Hampshire. I had a motorcycle to ride.

9

The first ride I took was to my mother's in Burlington, Vermont, 120 miles away. I hadn't ridden in a long time, and I was a little rusty, so I took the back roads. I continued to ride and ride and ride. I rode for work, going out to conduct quality and safety inspections on my bike. When I had to go to meetings in other parts of the state, I took my bike. I was taking it in for scheduled maintenance almost every other week. I took the beginning rider's course so I could get my motorcycle endorsement. I learned a lot and was much more comfortable on the bike after that. I took a couple of weeks off work and did a 1,700 mile loop around New England and New York by myself. By the time winter rolled in, I had over 10,000 miles on the bike.

I was in a constant battle in my job as a first line supervisor to union employees. While most of the installation and repair technicians were good people individually, the mob mentality would take over, and they worked harder to get out of work than to just do it. I was trying to keep my boss happy, but that meant getting these guys to cooperate at least a little bit. I was expected to do it by force if I had to, but going on a campaign of written warnings would get me nowhere except grievance meetings. I wasn't asking for too much, but nothing was going to make these guys appreciate their high-paying jobs in a rural area where most people earned half as much. Every conversation resulted in a confrontation. I know that without a union, the company would take advantage of their employees, but there had to be some middle ground where everyone could work together without the constant adversity. Unfortunately that wasn't the case. Even when I was off work, I was constantly trying to figure out how to handle every insignificant situation that popped up so it wouldn't become a big situation. I wasn't experienced or callous enough to leave the angst at the garage. Every waking hour was work for me, and I finally felt that no amount of money was worth it. I left the phone company for a job at the Harley dealership. Worst career move ever.

It never occurred to me that an employer, a small business owner in a small city, would be less than honest about a job description and salary. I was surprised that a business owner would place blame on others for decisions she made. Any attempt to take initiative was promptly squashed. I was glad I was no longer in the pit of vipers at the phone company, but I was in just as bad a place at the dealership only with half the pay.

As I was transitioning from one job to the other, Darren moved in with me. He bought the same exact bike that I had, only a year newer. We started talking about marriage. At 40, Darren had never been married, and it was a big deal for his parents. I was told to register for engagement party gifts, which I thought was absurd. I was 40 years old and owned my home. I didn't need any household items. A big lobster and clambake was set for the 4th of July weekend, and everyone was invited. Before the big day, Darren lost his job. While I was at my miserable job at the dealership, he stayed home all day looking for a job. Nothing was panning out. I'd come home and be faced with all the household chores. This was hugely stressful for me, since I was now making half what I had been at the phone company. Darren didn't have the same sense of urgency. He had a much better relationship with his parents and was able to count on them for financial assistance when needed. I had no desire to become dependent on them.

The day for the big party arrived. Relatives of mine that I hadn't seen in years showed up. I guess it's hard to resist a lobster dinner and free booze on the Maine coast in the summer. There was an absurd number of presents, none of which were requested, wanted or needed. Imagine the joy I felt when contemplating the task of writing thank you notes. Before I'd started writing, I was done. Instead of writing thank you notes, I was writing thank you, but the wedding is off, what do you want me to do with the gift, notes. Darren and his family felt it was on me to return all the gifts that I didn't want to begin with. I thought they should be happy that I promptly returned the two-carat diamond ring without making them fight for it.

I gave the gifts to Darren to redistribute in Maine, but there were a few left over. A lovely thick glass hurricane lamp had not come with a card indicating who it was from, so I kept that. There were also two amazing bath towels that were now used. Those stayed. My younger brother had given me a very colorful and interesting set of candlestick holders, and he told me to hang on to those. My older brother told me he was proud of me, that he'd have just gone ahead with the marriage and been miserable for the rest of his life. I had fought too hard for my freedom to allow that to happen.

While that relationship was at the end of its life, the director of the Harley Owners Group (HOG) chapter was hitting on me at the dealership. I thought he was married and ignored him for a while. It turned out he was recently divorced. We started hanging out, and I found I really liked him. Steve was an officer with the fire department. He'd been there forever and was well respected in town. I'd been trying to learn to quilt on my own, and it turned out that Steve's mother and several sisters were all quilters. The owner of the dealership couldn't stand him. It was perfect.

One day as I was leaving for work, I discovered I had a flat rear tire on my motorcycle. I called Steve for help, and he promptly showed up with a compressed air tank. We filled the tire, and he followed me down the road. It was a fast leak, and I didn't make it far before I was wobbling all over the road. More air. I made it to a small church before the bike got squirrely again. This time Steve refused to let me go on. He told me to stay put while he went and got a trailer. While loading the bike on the trailer, we had our first kiss. After that, August 9th was known as "Flat Tire Day."

It wasn't long before Steve wanted me to move in with him. I was a little hesitant since he had custody of his eight-year-old grandson. I had just spent 11 years raising my son with no help at all, and I didn't want to start over. Steve insisted that I wouldn't have to take any responsibility if I didn't want to. I was going to need to sell my house, so I went along with it.

Apparently Steve assumed that once I moved in, I'd be so in love with his grandson that we could disregard the statement about me not taking responsibility for a young child. Because Steve worked a lot of nights and weekends, most of the boy's care fell on me. I'd only had my bike for two seasons, and I had every intention of riding it as much as I wanted. But there I was, tied down to someone else's child against my will. I didn't have the problem with that particular child. Any child would have elicited the same reaction.

I loved Steve. We had a lot of fun together. We went to Harley-Davidson's 100th Anniversary celebration in Milwaukee together and rode in the parade, representing our HOG chapter. It was an incredible experience. We took other great rides, but the miles I traveled on my bike dropped considerably since I now had to care for a kid while Steve worked. I lived for the every-other-weekend that he'd be at his father's, but it was never long enough. Everything revolved around when he had to be picked up, reminding me of the days when I had to rush to daycare to get Dan before the clock struck 6:00. I'd had no help with Dan, and I wasn't getting a lot of help with Steve's grandson.

We got engaged. We got unengaged. Steve had two ex-wives who had cheated on him, and he was extremely suspicious. This didn't mesh well with my fear of being trapped, since it didn't take much for him to believe I was cheating on him. We went to counseling, which is where I gave the ring back to him. Although we were engaged, I wasn't allowed to discuss wedding plans at all. There was no date set. I told him to give the ring back when he was sure he wanted to marry me. Our biggest roadblock was that I did not love his grandson like he was my own child. Of course Steve hated Dan's presence in my life, and I was angry about the hypocrisy.

I started to regret having returned the ring. One day we were riding through Evans Notch, a stunning scenic ride that followed the state line between Maine and New Hampshire. It was a hot day, and we stopped at the river to cool off. Steve was digging around in some rocks and then came to me, presenting me with a gold colored fishing lure he'd found. He told me it was representative of the ring. He wanted to give the ring back, but there were conditions. I couldn't talk about the wedding for six months, and it would be at least two years before we were married. I was a little hurt by the conditions, but I laughed it off and agreed.

Six months put it right at Christmas. I figured I'd give it a week or two before I said anything. I finally worked up the nerve to talk about wedding plans.

"Just because you're allowed to talk about the wedding doesn't mean you have to."

It stung. I brought up the wedding date, which would be two years from the day at the river.

"No. It's two years from the time you were allowed to talk about the wedding. In December."

"But we should have the wedding in summer so we can go on a honeymoon on our motorcycles."

"Exactly. That gives me even more time."

I didn't bring up the subject again, but I wasn't giving the ring back this time. Steve was working a ton of overtime since one of the captains had recently retired, and the other was out on medical leave. That left me with a lot of babysitting. Steve was bringing home new toys for himself to the tune of $400 - $500 a couple of times a week. I was struggling to pay my bills. I felt like the hired help.

I attempted to get trained for a second job while living with Steve. The State of New Hampshire wanted me to train as a motorcycle instructor. Steve and I went to Concord for their try-outs, and they liked me. Steve had serious issues with anyone telling him what to do, and he didn't like the idea that these guys would be directing me during training. They acted like professionals, but Steve hated the whole idea. I started to go through the training anyway, but then Steve told me that if I was working on a weekend, he was taking off on the bike without me. This didn't sit well since I was not allowed to ride without him without generating suspicion, followed by a huge argument. I finally gave up the idea, because Steve is really good at making life miserable if he didn't get his way. In addition to the lack of support from Steve, I also felt like a hypocrite. I don't like to wear a helmet, and there is a huge emphasis on protective gear in the class.

Steve wasn't awful by any means. He was the hardest-working person I've ever been with, but he still took time to relax and enjoy riding and baseball games. He took me out to dinner often and helped me pay my vehicle registration fees one time when I was worried about that. He also paid for our vacations without a second thought. He was often in the paper for some heroic deed done on the job with the fire department, and everyone loved him. I always felt so comfortable with him and loved him dearly. I've compared every relationship I've had since then to how I felt with Steve. But Steve made me realize that just because two people love each other, it doesn't mean they should be married.

We were planning a ride on the Blue Ridge Parkway at the end of May. At the beginning of April, before I was leaving for work, Steve told me he'd be going to Manchester that day to get some money out of his savings account. He had just put $5,000 down on a new tractor, and he wanted to maintain the cushion in his checking account. He might as well have slapped me in the face. Again, he couldn't have made that money without my help, but he never saw it like that. I suppose if I'd been joyous and happy in my caring for his grandson, he'd have felt differently. But because it was a struggle for me, it was as though I never did any of it.

Two engagements down, but this time I left with the ring. Steve couldn't understand why I was upset. The fact that I'd spent all of my free time raising his grandson while he raked in the dough didn't appear offensive to him. The fact that I had no extra money while giving him the opportunity to earn six figures that year meant nothing. He graciously told me that if anything happened to him, he was sure his family would allow me to stay in the house for a couple of months. Although I was going to have trouble making ends meet, I couldn't stay any longer.

I went on the Blue Ridge Parkway ride by myself. I visited my Godmother on Long Island, a friend on the Jersey Shore, and then took the ferry to Delaware. I continued down the East Coast to Virginia Beach where I turned and cut across North Carolina to Murphy, a place very close to where I'd lived with Jimmy. Steve and I were trying to work things out. Because he was still insecure about other men, I spoke to no one. I covered over 3,000 miles in about 10 days, took lots of pictures, and didn't really enjoy myself. I'd made reservations at campgrounds before I went, so I was forced to keep plugging along, even if I wanted to rest, or forced to stop, even if I wanted to go on. I felt like a nun with a vow of silence. Before long, Steve and I ended the relationship completely.

I wanted to get back into the motorcycle instructor training that I'd ended before it ever started. Because the state had paid for me to take it and I backed out before (I'd never had any training, but I was signed up for it), they wouldn't pay for it again. After some deliberation, the trainers accepted me into their next class. I was very grateful for that, although that gratitude was short-lived once I started the class. Kidding, really. I am still very grateful, but nothing could have prepared me for the extreme nature of the class.

I was working at the college full time, enrolled in two classes for my MBA program, and now I was taking the training. I hadn't known there'd be so much homework in the training class. There was no mercy for errors of any kind. Every step was noted, analyzed and criticized. There were three people in the class from New Hampshire and three from Massachusetts.

The two states handled training in different ways. Anyone in Massachusetts could get the training as long as they wanted to cough up the tuition for the class. New Hampshire paid for the class, but there was a screening process before they did that. It quickly became apparent that the New Hampshire students were far more focused than the folks from the south. The woman from Mass dropped out of the class, and then there were five of us. It was tough. It was the first time in my life that I wasn't sure I would pass a class. I came out at the top of my class and was the only one who rode my motorcycle every time we met, but the training was brutal. Regardless, teaching riding as a part time job sure beat picking up work at JC Penney.

I missed Steve, especially when I had to drive by the firehouse, which was a few times a day. I lived downtown now, in a big house that had been broken up into several apartments. I had left my weights at his house, and I e-mailed to ask that he bring them over. He waited until he thought I'd gone to work and brought them by. He didn't know that I'd purchased a new (used) car and was there when he arrived. I helped unload the weights, and he never said a word. I couldn't tell if he was angry or sad.

During that winter, I started making plans to go on a cross-country trip. While attempting to deal with life as a custodial step-grandmother, I'd become involved with a stepmother support website whose members often met for get-togethers. I'd met a few of the women already and considered one of them, Gigi, to be one of my closest friends. One of the ladies in Truckee, California was planning a party at the end of July. I decided I would ride my bike out there for the event. I'd left the dealership in the beginning of my relationship with Steve, and by this time, I'd been working at the college for a few years. I'd been there long enough to have the vacation and personal days available to pull it off. At first I planned a straight out and back route that would take about ten days. I was excited. I never thought I'd be one of those people who could make a ride like that. Not because of my skills or endurance, but because of time and money.

I did a little more calculating with the vacation time, and decided that since I was going all the way out there, I should detour for some scenic rides as well. The plan morphed into 23 days through 27 states and over 8,000 miles. I was doing it by myself. I was concerned about finances, and my bike had at least 60,000 miles on it by then, but I felt as though it was now or never, and I kept on with the plan.

In early spring, I took my first ride of the season. As I was approaching the town green, the traffic light in front of the firehouse turned red. While I was waiting at the light, one of the fire trucks was stopped at the intersection to my left. I couldn't tell if Steve was in it, but when my light turned green and I crossed in front of the engine, Steve waved.

I got an e-mail from Steve shortly after that. It had been a year since I left, and we hadn't spoken at all. He was involved with a woman he felt was a little psycho, and he was worried about making her mad since she owed him some money. He'd done a ton of work on Tina's house and put a few new appliances on his credit card. I don't know if she loved him, but she certainly used him and probably didn't want to lose her source of free labor and interest-free credit.

We started seeing each other a little, but he remained nervous about Tina. This irritated me, because he never worried about what other people thought. One day I arrived at the Harley dealership to help lead demo rides, and I saw the ambulance at the gas station next door. I peeked over the hill and saw Steve filling it up. I walked over the hill, thinking he'd be happy to see me and give me a hug and a kiss, but all I got was a wave with his hand not going above his waist. I don't think Tina worked at the station, but she knew a lot of people there, and Steve was afraid word would get back. Even though Steve claimed to have ended it with Tina, he was acting as though we were having an illicit affair. Steve finally got his money back from her and stopped worrying about the girl. She was already moving on to another sugar daddy.

Steve and I eased back into the relationship. I was still planning my ride beginning in the middle of July, and he was planning on doing a ride out west with the International Association of Fire Fighters (IAFF) motorcycle group. He wanted me to go with him. I appreciated his desire to include me, but I really wanted to go on my own trip, and I couldn't do both. I tossed around options for a while, and eventually made the decision: I was going on my own. Steve was not happy with this, and by the time I left, we weren't speaking.

10

As I prepared for my journey, I had a persistent feeling that my life was going to change. I wrapped up all of my affairs as though I wasn't coming back. It was exciting and a little eerie at the same time. With the help of some coworkers, I created a blog so I could write about the trip as I traveled. I made sure I had room for my MacBook in the saddlebag. I knew I'd be camping out a lot, but I figured I'd find enough electricity on the road to keep the computer going. As it turned out, the blog helped friends and family keep up with me, but it wasn't so good because I couldn't tell stories when I got back. Everyone already knew all the events of the trip.

Except for Steve, all of my readers loved the blog. They said it felt as though they were on the trip with me. Steve said it sounded like a complaint log. What I learned on the trip is that you can't have a good story without adversity, so if someone just looked at the blog as a list of what was difficult or what went wrong, then yes, it was a complaint log.

Thankfully most people looked at for what I meant it to be: the journal of a woman riding a Harley-Davidson across the country by herself.

I expected that as a person crosses the country, cultures change, and conversations about the same subject would alter somewhat. But put a woman on a loaded up Harley-Davidson, by herself, and the response is standard:

"Where are you from?"

"New Hampshire."

"Where are you going?"

"Back to New Hampshire, eventually."

"Are you travelling by yourself?"

"Yes."

"You're very brave."

"No, just crazy."

As the trip continued on, my mind wandered on the subject, and I thought of all the brave Americans who had fought and died or permanently impacted in some way to keep our country free. Those are the brave ones, not me. And I continued on... Free. Freedom. Freedom isn't free. Over a year later, I was watching an episode of

"Sons of Anarchy", when the narrator spoke a piece on freedom. It included the following:

> *"True freedom requires sacrifice and pain. Most human beings only think they want freedom. In truth they yearn for the bondage of social order, rigid laws and materialism. The only freedom man really wants... is the freedom to be comfortable."*

Sitting in your living room, anticipating the next season of American Idol, is not what Americans fought and died for – at least not in my mind. In my life, I've had the freedom to make some really bad decisions and then dig myself out of those holes. I've had the freedom to attend meetings in church basements to give myself another chance. Freedom to travel across the country on my motorcycle, choosing the roads, the ending point for that day, and choosing to handle whatever Mother Nature had to throw at me or finding a dry overpass – those are some of the freedoms I find most important. This is the United States. We have good roads and the citizens are typically law-abiding. What I was doing didn't involve bravery; I was practising freedom.

The trip changed my life. I knew it would, but it happened in a way I never expected. This is the story...

Tuesday, June 19, 2007

Gearing up! Leaving on July 20th.

I've been considering this trip since January. I made some preliminary plans, but now it's time to work out a route. I'd like to be a lot more flexible, but I also want to see friends along the way. I'd like to be able to give them a vague idea of when I'll be visiting. I found a feature on the Harley-Davidson (or was it HOG?) website today that lists "great rides". I'm going to have to ride the Beartooth Highway, and I'll have to find a few more. I'm sure there are at least one or two scenic cruises between New Hampshire and California.

And no, that's not a stock color

My bike is a 2001 Harley-Davidson Softail not-so-Standard. I've got almost 60,000 miles on it, all of which I've put on in the last 6 years. OK, I think Steve (ex-fiance and now a good friend) may have ridden it about 10 miles, and the guy that put on my new tires last probably put on 20 miles between his place and mine. It was Vivid Black when I bought it new. It quickly became Vivid Swirly Marks and impossible to keep looking nice. I like to joke that I change the color of my bike as often as I change the color of my hair, but honestly, hair color is only about $8 a box and 45 minutes of my time. Changing the color of my bike is considerably more of both.

I thought about buying a Road King Custom a few years back. I love the way that bike looks and I can always use more cargo space for the long rides, but I was afraid I'd miss the feel of my Softail. Another thing I joke about is that I've been married to two rigid frame, suicide clutch Panheads - their owners anyway. It's a miracle I still have a spine. But that's what I "grew up" on, and I like the way they sit. Besides, I've put so much into my bike and it's my best friend. I could never get rid of it. Someday I'll have the money and the garage space for a second bike - and who knows what I'll want by then. For now I've settled for the Road King Custom tank emblems.

THURSDAY, JUNE 28, 2007

I'm ready

I'm going to need new tires at some point, but I don't want to replace them until I really need to. No sense wasting all that tread. I'm thinking about calling ahead to a dealership out west and making an appointment for new tires and an oil change when I get there. The only problem is that I'd like to be a little flexible on my time - 24 hours plus or minus. I'll probably give a call and see what they suggest. I'm sure I'm not the first person who's ever been in this situation.

TUESDAY, JULY 3, 2007

I think I have the route down

I've put everything into the ride planner. I'll be posting the route back home shortly. I got some advice on a route to Albuquerque from a Harley rider on a bike talk forum. I'm doing some of that route, which takes me across Nevada and into Utah. I'm detouring from his suggestion to hit a couple of "Great Roads" from Harley's website. This will take me to the edge of the Grand Canyon. I hadn't planned on stopping there, but as long as it can be on the way, why not? Before that I'll be driving "Highway 12 - A Journey Through Time Scenic Byway" in southern Utah. The name isn't exciting, but the photos are stunning.

I'm looking forward to a couple of days in a hotel in Albuquerque while visiting with a friend from the stepmom support site (SMS) and her family. I have some free nights coming from LaQuinta, and since my friend has convinced me that a campground in ABQ is not safe, that's where I'll use them.

I made plans to ride the Tail of the Dragon during the last few days of the trip. I was having a hard time figuring out how to fit it into my route, so I e-mailed the folks at tailfothedragon.com and they got back to me immediately with the information I needed. I found a campground on their website, Hunt's Lodge Motorcycle Campground, and I spoke to one of the owners. He told me that one day wasn't enough, but I'm really just passing through quickly because I missed it last year when I rode the Blue Ridge Parkway. It wasn't on purpose.

THURSDAY, JULY 12, 2007

That's never happened before

Something woke me up in the middle of the night last night. I started worrying about the trip. Am I going to be ready? Can I afford it? Am I going make it? Being ready and affording it I can understand, but being nervous about the trip itself? Very strange. I couldn't get back to sleep so I got up and did a few things on my list. I looked for my second camera battery but couldn't find it. I did get the cord so I can download pics along the way. In my PC I have an SD slot, but I don't have that in the MacBook. I hadn't used the cord before and it worked perfectly. I also dug out my teeny tripod and put that with my pile of stuff to go. I got back to sleep and in the light of day I was fine. I'm unable to recreate that doubt, not that I want to. Good thing.

I dropped the bike off at the dealership at lunch time so they can go over it. I told them not to find anything expensive. I've been doing all the maintenance on my bike, so I guess the dealer never thought to mention that I should have my cam shoes (whatever those are) checked out. Apparently when those go, the timing in the motor is gone and bad things happen. I remember a sculpture I used to have back in the day. It was a valve embedded in a piston. Not a good thing to happen at any time, let alone a long way from home. Hopefully they'll pull the cam cover off and it will look as good as the day I bought it.

I'm supposed to be leading my Old Man of the Mountain memorial ride on Saturday. The weather doesn't look like it's going to cooperate. It has rained a lot lately. I hope it's more sunny on my trip, but on the other hand, it's been so hot and dry out west that everything's burning. Can you put a smoke detector in a tent?

THURSDAY, JULY 12, 2007 (second entry)

Whew!

The cam shoes are worn but not critical. I wasn't expecting them to look at the bike until tomorrow, but I got a voice mail while I was shooting that said it was all done. Since they didn't call to have me approve any work, I guess it was all good. The guy I've been teaching the Basic Rider Course with the last couple of weekends called and asked how it went. I told him I had been hoping that it was an issue with the 88A motors and not the 88Bs. I still don't know, but as long as everything is looking good on mine, I'm happy.

I was awesome at 5-stand tonight! I'm finally getting it. I was starting to feel like I was just throwing my money away. Shotgun ammo is not cheap. No ammo is, but each round of 5-stand is $5 (at least) of ammunition plus the $5 to shoot the round. The guys have been helpful and working with me and I started reading a book to help out. It's starting to pay off. It feels great when those targets explode. Of course now I'll be going on my trip and won't shoot for another month.

FRIDAY, JULY 13, 2007

That's my bottom end you're talking about!

I must not have heard the whole voice mail message. They haven't finished going through the bike yet. I found that out after my neighbor dropped me off at the dealership at 7:30 this morning. Even though the cam shoes are OK, the lobes on the cams are starting to look a little worn. The service writer told me that the mechanic working on the bike, another mechanic, and he all looked at it. I felt violated. It was like going in for a gyn exam and while you're there with your feet up in the stirrups, the doc decides to go grab a couple of his friends to have a look. Hey! That's my bottom end. Keep it to yourself buddy. You can't just show my cam lobes to anyone.

So the bike hasn't had the once over yet. The owner gave me the loaner minivan to get to work. Nice gesture, but I would have preferred the Street Glide.

TUESDAY, JULY 17, 2007

I think I'm ready

I was getting nervous about not being ready to go, but I'm feeling good now. I got a lot of paperwork done last night. All the bills are caught up. I changed the oil in the bike on Sunday and inspected the primary chain. I even washed my floors before work this morning. I want the house to be clean when I get home. I still need to construct the clear vinyl pouch to hold the book of directions I had made from the Ride Planner.

I printed the ride planner output to a pdf document and then copied and pasted the stuff I wanted into a Word document. Every day has the proposed mileage, how long it should take at the posted speed limit, directions (edited), maps, and all the Harley dealerships within 10 miles of my route (reverse Murphy's law - if I'm prepared for a breakdown, it won't happen). I printed it out with two pages to one, then took it the copy place and had them laminate it into a small spiral bound book. It's really cool. I'm making this clear pouch that will go on my tank panel and hold the book so I'll have the directions right there. I don't mind stopping to check out a map on a 200 mile day, but on those 400 - 500 mile days I'd rather just get on through.

WEDNESDAY, JULY 18, 2007

33 hours to go

I hate to bring this up, but where better than in a blog? I'd like to take a handgun with me, but it wouldn't be legal in most states. I've never been a fan of gun control, but I've never felt quite so affected or offended by it before. There are a lot of creeps out there just waiting to come across some vulnerable woman and take her down. I don't consider myself at risk. I've had 6 years of martial arts training, I shoot skeet and 5-stand, I'm an ice hockey player, and I ride my own Harley. I'm tall and strong and not easily intimidated. But I feel I should have the right to carry a handgun with me in case someone who can't find an easier target decides I'm it. But that would be against the law and I could go to jail for that. Does this make sense? I'm sure there are arguments against this, but I would like to have some responsibility for my own safety. Does this mean I shouldn't ride around our great country by myself? Does it mean I should stay inside and lock the doors because there are evil people out there? I don't think so. This is my country and I should not have to limit my freedom out of fear.

FRIDAY, JULY 20, 2007

Miles 0 to 516

The day started out good, quickly went to Hell in a hand basket, and ended up spectacular. I stopped in Woodstock (VT) for breakfast at the Wasp diner. My son knows the people who own it, and I've heard interesting things about the place. Very friendly and not in a hokey way. Lots of fun, interesting customers and great food. My fried egg turned out to be a double-yolker! I was told it was good luck and assumed that meant it wouldn't rain the rest of the day. Wrong.

The weather turned nasty over Killington. I stopped to put on rain gear before I started up the mountain. Almost to the top everything got very dark, very quickly, and visibility was just about nil. It was raining, of course, and the wind was whipping me all over the place. Fortunately the weather improved on the other side, but not greatly. The wind was destined to stick with me the whole time. I feel like I've been fighting invisible gnomes who have been trying to pull my bike out from under me all day. The rain continued sporadically until some point on I-90. I finally felt it was safe to take the rain gear off and stopped at the next rest area. It was about 2:00.

Unlike last year's solo trip, were I was under strict orders from the boyfriend to not talk to strangers, I can socialize. Freedom! I chatted with some guys from Ontario and then went into the facility. I heard some other bikers discussing the whereabouts of local Harley dealerships. Well I just happened to have my handy book I made for the trip, still enclosed in the handy vinyl pouch that attaches to my tank panel. I pulled it out and one guy said he'd seen those pouches before. No, probably not like this one. I told him I had made it.

Then I pulled the book out of the panel and this incredibly handsome guy says that I probably made the book too. Yep. Then he asks if I'm married. Nope. Do you want to get married? LOL. Marriage is a little more than I'm looking for right now. We all laughed, looked up dealerships and I went on my way. So already I've had more fun and interaction than my whole 3,000 mile trip last year.

I was worried that I wouldn't want to go the full 449 miles in the plan, but I was feeling fine. I pushed it past Erie, PA and got a campsite off of exit 18. The owners are very friendly. They told me where a car wash was, good restaurants, and a killer sunset. I washed the bike and stopped at this great little pizza place called McKean Pizza in, well, McKean as the name would suggest. There was a Softail out front, which belongs to the owner's little brother. Once again, it was a very friendly place and it seemed like all the customers were family. Good food too. After I left there I noticed that there really was going to be an amazing sunset so I blasted to the beach, hoping I could get there before the sun dropped below the horizon. I made it and took lots of pictures. Beautiful!

I'm glad I got the extra miles in. That will make it easier tomorrow. I can get to BG's (another SMS friend) earlier and spend more time with her, rather than having to sneak in after dark and make an attempt at not waking the baby.

SATURDAY, JULY 21, 2007

516 to 1,000

I got up early and packed up. I wasn't too worried about waking up the families with the children that were up screeching until after midnight. It seemed to be slow getting out of the gate. Breakfast, go a few miles, gas, go a few miles, Harley dealership, go a few miles, gas again. Ugh. It was chilly in the morning. I really wasn't in a groove and I was getting irritated with feeling so out of sorts. Finally, coming into Cleveland, it all came together. I didn't expect Cleveland to work for me like that. I guess it was early enough. The lake was beautiful, the air was clear, the roads were smooth. The city looked so clean and quiet and peaceful, although I know it was just an illusion. I haven't heard much good about Cleveland.

I tried listening to my iPod while riding. My bike is just too loud. It worried me that I had to crank the volume almost all the way to hear anything over my engine, and then it was just bits and pieces. Oh well. I like the sound of my bike.

At some point during this day I started thinking about Forrest Gump and him running back and forth across the country. I keep thinking I'm going to end up back home looking as disheveled as he did at the end of his run. I thought of all my friends cheering me on: Run Forrest, run! I stopped at a service area (I do often. I'm getting about 25 miles per gallon) and was talking with a group of Harley riders. They were three couples from Ohio on their way to South Dakota. I told them about my trip and my blog and he asked if I felt like Forrest Gump. As a matter of fact, I do! I brought along a stack of my Old Man of the Mountain memorial patches to give out when the mood struck me, and it struck me at that point. I gave them all a patch, which then segued into a reason for the minister of the group to call for a prayer. I'm not religious. I've given it some thought from time to time, but I wasn't brought up in a God loving household, so it's never been very natural for me. I have to say, I wasn't at all put out by his request and was more than happy to stand in the circle holding hands and having a prayer said for me and my safety on the trip. And good timing too! Just after the service area I got onto I-80 in Gary, Indiana and I was real happy that I'd been prayed for at the last stop. Crazy traffic. That kind where it's bumper to bumper at 80 miles per hour and all it takes is one squirrel making a bad decision to really fuck up everyone's day.

Along here sometime I realized that I didn't have BG's phone number and I wanted to let her know about when I'd be arriving. I called Cheryl, another SMS friend, and asked her to send BG a private message and let her know - assuming she would even be on Stepmom Station. Well then I realized that I didn't have BG's street number, just the directions to her road. Doh. I had to call Gigi to call Gina to see if she could get the information and call me back. She did, she did, and she did. I found the house, minutes after losing a taillight lens thanks to a pothole. BG's children were adorable, I slept like a rock, and got out of there on Sunday morning.

SUNDAY, JULY 22, 2007

1000 - to around 1490

I stopped to get something to eat after leaving BG's house. I opened the card she gave me. I was almost crying! It was my Throw Flowers Off a Bridge Day present. Very sweet. Throw Flowers Off a Bridge Day replaced Flat Tire Day last year. Flat Tire Day was the anniversary of my first kiss with Steve. Throw Flowers Off a Bridge Day has to do with getting over things that Flat Tire Day celebrated. Better to have loved and lost, right? And wouldn't ya know, the day will hit during my trip - August 9th, to be exact. I think I'll be on the Tail of the Dragon that day. And I'll have to find some flowers to throw off a bridge.

I stopped at Capitol City Harley-Davidson in Madison, WI to get a lens for my taillight. $8. Unbelievable. It's a small piece of plastic. I also made the decision to buy for a t-shirt quilt. They have a sharp custom t-shirt back that I couldn't live without. And so the collecting begins.

I met Julie for lunch at a truck stop in Mauston. It was a quick lunch, but it was good to see her and have a chance to chat for a few minutes. I got a little stressed as I got close to the state line. My jacket was driving me crazy. The wind gets in it and pushes up in my neck and chin and face. I stopped at the dealership near LaCrosse to see if they had something with zippers that would keep the jacket from puffing up. The dealership is right next to the interstate, but it was impossible to find off the exit. By the time I found it they were closed. I got there about 2 minutes too late. That's fine. I'm sure I saved myself at least a hundred bucks. A guy there was showing some other riders how to get back to the interstate so I tagged along.

I forgot that I meant to stop and get gas there and was stressing about it as we crossed the Mississippi. I jumped off at the next exit, stupidly assuming that because every exit in the state of Wisconsin had gas this one would. Nope. I went down a little farther and got some. At this point the clouds were rolling in and it was looking like I was going to be pitching my tent in the rain. I just kept cruising along and eventually broke through the menacing weather. My goal was Austin. I blew by that exit with plenty of riding left in me. I stopped for dinner and was horrified at the rat's nest my hair had become. I unbraided it and spent half an hour getting all the knots out. Ouch. Back on the road and I got more than 100 miles past my goal. I'm now enjoying the pool, the laundry facilities and the wireless internet access at a KOA in Jackson, MN. Rapid City tomorrow!

MONDAY, JULY 23, 2007

1490 – 1938

It was 110 degrees today, which didn't count the 88 cubic inch motor between my legs. I've never ridden in heat like that before. I'm sure it didn't help that it was wide-open interstate. I'd be riding along and just when I'd start not thinking about how miserable I was, a blast of hot air would practically knock me off my bike. The whole way across South Dakota there were big round bales of hay. I kept expecting them to burst into a ball of flames. I could barely get 50 miles before stopping.

I stopped first thing at the dealership in Sioux Falls because my rear brake pedal suddenly dropped. Not all the way, but very noticeable. They didn't find anything wrong with it, so I was quickly on my way.

I ran into my new Christian friends from Gary, Indiana first thing in the morning. I told them that I was happy they had prayed for me just before I got on I-80 in Indiana because I had really needed it. They agreed that it was treacherous. I ran into them a little later and one of the women told me how she was dousing her husband with water to keep him cool. As we crossed the state, separate but always taking a break at the same place. I'm concerned that my life-changing experience on this trip will be that I find God. How lame is that?

I took a cue from the woman and decided I'd start bathing in cold water. I couldn't do it while riding, but when I stopped I'd buy a bottle of cold water and pour it over my head. I was trying to be discreet about it since I didn't want to look like I was trying to pull off some middle-aged wet t-shirt stunt. It was working out just fine until my last stop about 20 miles before Rapid City. There was a cowboy sitting in a big red pickup truck right next to my bike. I was hoping he'd leave, but he didn't. I talked to him about the weather and then poured the bottle of water over my head. I was bone dry in less than 10 miles.

It seems to be cooling down now. I'm at the campsite. I had dinner delivered since I couldn't stand the thought of getting back on the bike after a shower. I'm now in the mountain time zone, so it's only about 8:15 here. I wish I could sleep the rest of the night off right now. It's supposed to be hot again tomorrow, but now I'll be starting in the fun and scenic portion of the trip, with many less miles planned, so I'm optimistic that it will be more bearable. If it's going to be this hot when I leave Albuquerque, I'll probably head back up to Colorado and east from there.

TUESDAY, JULY 24, 2007

1938 – 2205

I slept really well last night, despite the heat. It must have taken a lot out of me. The thing about campgrounds is that whatever is going on around you is your life too - like the inconsolable baby sometime in the middle of the night. The campground was OK, but wasn't nearly as comfortable as the one in MN. This one was outside of Rapid City.

I got up early and took off for the Black Hills right away. I wasn't too sure if I had good plans to see the countryside. I stopped at a store to get something to eat and started talking to a group of retired men hanging out there. They were friendly and happy to help me find my way. I hadn't gone very far when I saw a store that sold Christmas stuff. Not a draw for me, but the other half of the sign said, "Quilt Corral - Fun and fabulous fabrics". You can't say "fun and fabulous fabrics" and not expect me to stop. I guess that's the point. It was a great store, and once I determined that they'd send my purchases home, well that was all I needed to hear. They even had "Camo Girls", a new favorite of the Grafton County Fish and Game Association. I picked up a Mt. Rushmore print and a few others I can't live without.

I rode on to Hill City, then to Mt. Rushmore. There was finally a good reason to get my camera out. After that was Iron Mountain Road. I loved the sign at the beginning of the road that warned of extremely twisty roads and small tunnels. There should have been one more thing on the sign: IF YOU'RE A PUSSY, STAY AWAY. I was practically walking my bike around some of the curves, thanks to the scared minivan drivers. Then there was the racy car with the spoiler that never got above 15. There should be requirements for buying a sports car - like you can't be afraid to drive.

I got on this tangent in my thinking while idling through the curves. It was so hot that the asphalt was not quite a solid. My parched brain started thinking about a combination of the Virtual Terrorism Response Academy and the poison line and the physical properties of things. My mind turned the threshold limit value (TLV) into a temperature rather than a concentration. Then I was trying to determine the melting point of blacktop and figured there must be a TLV where the asphalt becomes immediately dangerous to life and health (IDLH). It sounds goofy now, but extreme heat can do strange things to your mind.

Needles Highway was after that, and once again there were many very slow drivers. At least most of these people had the consideration to pull over when they could to let people pass. After that was a ride through Deadwood and on to Spearfish Canyon. This was probably my favorite part of the day. Spectacular views; not just natural, but some beautiful log cabins throughout. All that took up most of the day and I needed to get going to Buffalo, Wyoming.

Once I was out of the canyon the heat became unbearable again. A sign in downtown Spearfish said 111 degrees. I was getting back on I-90 at that point and was starting to have flashbacks from the previous day. I didn't have too far to go. When I stopped for gas I noticed that the temperature gauge on my oil tank said 200 degrees. While this may not be entirely accurate, it is very high compared to what it usually runs at. I could have made it to Buffalo, but I was worried about my baby and decided to call it a day in Gillette. I was even going to spring for a hotel room. The Motel 6 was a whopping $89! So I'm at another campground (Crazy Lady Campground - appropriate, eh?). I think there's some big rodeo going on here in town and all the hotels are full, as is the campground.

Washed clothes again because I'll be damned if I'm going to put on a pair of black jeans and a black t-shirt tomorrow. Speaking of t-shirts, I'll have a nice quilt going when I get home. Stocking up.

Hoping for some cooler weather tomorrow. I looked at weather.com and I'm in the hottest spot in the country right now.

Wednesday, July 25

2205-2520

Last night was a little scary. Very windy. I have a fear of tornadoes. I'm not sure that I've ever heard of tornadoes in Wyoming, but there's always a chance, right? The wind finally died down and then I learned that my campground neighbor was a guy who giggles. Camping like that is like living in an apartment with very thin walls.

Something really bizarre happened in my first mile. I was just about at the entrance to I-90 when something hit me in the stomach. I looked down and this bird was flopping around in my lap. About this time, two trucks were passing in the opposite direction. I know those drivers will think about the look on my face and the bird frantically trying to get away and laugh their asses off for months. I was horrified. The bird was just spinning around, flapping its wings and freaking out. I was trying to keep the bike upright while trying to figure out how to get this ball of feathers, claws and a beak out of my personal space. It finally managed to get on its way with no help from me.

Within another minute or two I realized I should have filled up the gas tank before I got on the highway. The exits were few and far between. I stopped at the next exit that had gas, only to find that there wasn't any premium. I bought a gallon of regular unleaded to get me to Buffalo, Wyoming, where I planned on getting off the interstate and onto a more scenic road. I stopped for gas and to get a snack for breakfast. There were a couple of other Harley riders there and we talked for a while. They were headed the same way - west on Highway 16 towards Cody. We talked about the heat of the last couple of days, and then discussed the need to put a jacket on before venturing into the mountains. How refreshing! I took off with a wool zip-up shirt on, thinking that would be enough. Before too long I realized it wasn't and stopped to put my on my jacket. While I was stopped, the two guys passed me. A little while later, I passed them. We had that leapfrog thing going on. I stopped to take some pictures, and as I was pulling out, they passed me. We ended up riding together into the next town.

We all got some gasoline and talked about riding on to Cody together and getting lunch. After lunch we headed out the same way, but they were going to one end of the Beartooth Highway while I was going to the other end in Red Lodge, Montana. We hit a little rain, enough to stop and put our rain gear on. I didn't get too much rain after we parted ways, but it looks like they might have hit a good bit in the mountains.

I wimped out and got a hotel room tonight. I needed a break from the Thermarest and there were some pretty ominous clouds over Red Lodge. Besides, the hotel on the edge of town advertised a complimentary bike wash (hoses and wash rags), and I couldn't pass it up. So, sitting here typing and watching tv, it appears that a small plane crashed very close to where I was riding today, and there was a mudslide about 40 miles from Cody, on the edge of Yellowstone, which was caused by excessive rain. Tomorrow I'll be riding through Yellowstone and on to Pocatello, Idaho.

THURSDAY, JULY 26, 2007

2520 - 2844

The day didn't look too good to start, but it wasn't actively raining when I left the hotel. I saw a bunch of bikes heading up into the hills. I was slow getting started, so when I was ready to go I took off for the mountains myself, never thinking about gasoline. When I did think about it, I noticed I had about half a tank and a little over 60 miles to go on the Beartooth Highway. It was going to be close. I figured if I could make it to the top I could coast on the other side.

Unfortunately there was a lot of very low cloud cover. I did manage to get some beautiful shots, but I'll have to come back another time when it's clear. It got pretty cool near the top. Yesterday, when I stopped for gas the first time with the guys I'd met on the road, there was another guy who pulled up on a Harley and told us that there was snow up in the Beartooth Pass. I wouldn't have referred to it as snow. I think "glacier" is the term. No, I just looked it up on Wikipedia. Maybe it's permanent snow. Glacial would mean that it's moving, although not at a high rate of speed. You could define "glacial" as something similar to cage-driving tourists in the Black Hills and Yellowstone.

At any rate, there was some long-standing frozen stuff around. I stopped at a small store near the center of the highway and grabbed a cup of coffee. They had gas, which they sold by the half gallon, but the cashier told me it was 25 miles to Cooke City and I knew I could make that. I drank a cup of coffee and chatted with a foreign biker (foreign bike and biker with European accent) from Chicago. As he was getting up to leave, a group of Harleys pulled in. Turned out they were from New Hampshire! I got on the road myself, but ran into them again when I was finishing up lunch in Cooke City.

From there it was on to Yellowstone. $20 to get through the gate. Don't our federal taxes go to support national parks? That's a lot of money to get a motorcycle in. The Denali behind me, stuffed to the gills with screaming brats, only had to pay $5 more. Just doesn't seem right. I had not wanted to stop for pictures, but for that price, I was going to get my money's worth. It was very pretty and with some interesting vegetation.

Somewhere in the middle of Yellowstone traffic had stopped. My bike was getting hot and didn't want to run. There was a truck behind me and a group of Harley riders behind him. We had all shut down while waiting. There was a herd of buffalo around and we figured people were simply stopping in the middle of the road to take pictures. This is not unheard of. Turns out there where buffalo in the road and nobody could get by. At this point I got a little nervous, having heard that not too long ago a biker was airlifted out of the park (or maybe it was over in the Black Hills) after being charged by a buffalo while trying to ride through a herd in the road.

One of the bikers saw my New Hampshire license plate and asked if I'd rode all the way.

"Yes."

"By yourself?"

"Yes."

"My kind of woman!"

I figured there was some man out there that would feel that way, I just assumed he wouldn't have been on leave from the assisted living facility. Oh well. The buffalo finally moved and we got on our way. Not too long later it started raining and I put on the rain gear. Not too long after that I realized I was in for a lengthy and hearty rain and went to the yellow glasses and some gloves. I was about 80 miles from Jackson, Wyoming when it started. I quickly became unable to see. I had to pull the glasses down on my nose and tilt the visor of my helmet down and peek through this little slice of visibility. And that went on for the whole 80 miles.

I left Yellowstone and entered Grand Teton National Park. I've heard there are mountains there, but I couldn't testify to that. The only thing I saw was a white line and at least one yellow line, maybe some grass and trees on the fringe. Actually, a few miles outside of Jackson I saw an outline of some jagged peaks. I stopped and took a couple of pictures. They are mostly clouds with some vague outlines of mountains. As all this was going on, I decided it was going to be another hotel night. But not in Jackson. $115 for a sleazy motel? Uh-uh. I wasn't about to pay resort prices just so I could wake up and ride in the rain tomorrow. I made that mistake last year. I toughed it out to Idaho Falls - another 70 or so miles.

The ride between Jackson and Idaho Falls was beautiful. You go through the Teton Pass. I was worried that it would be long and cold like the Beartooth, but I was assured that it wasn't. A little chilly maybe, but it wasn't a long ride. While coming into Swan Valley, I saw a rainbow. Actually, it was more like a rain-segment. Regardless, it was a delight, as rainbows always are. That was just before I had to take a right hand turn into some of the most dreadful looking clouds I've seen yet. It didn't help that the color of the setting sun was getting in there, so we had these very low dark clouds tinged with orange. I really wanted to take a picture, but I wanted more to get the Hell out of there. Unfortunately I didn't move fast enough and got hit by some piercing rain. Good news was that it was within 20 miles of Idaho Falls, so I didn't have that far to ride in it.

I made it to the Super 8 (much nicer than last night's), jumped in the hot tub, then went out for dinner. Two nights in a row in a hotel. I'm getting spoiled. Just before I hit the second batch of rain, I was ready to camp out. But when that rain hit, I got tensed up so badly that I could not turn my head to the right. I was worried I was about to blow out a disc or something. I had to get into some hot water quickly. The hot tub was perfect. Tomorrow I'll be in the desert.

FRIDAY, JULY 27, 2007

2844 - 3301

In the light of a bright and sunny morning, I saw what I expected - a really nasty, dirty motorcycle. I waited until the local dealership was opening and stopped by to pick up a Grand Teton Harley-Davidson t-shirt for the quilt and asked to borrow a hose to wash the bike. They washed it for me! I'll be damned. It took a little while since there were a couple ahead of mine, but no problem. It's a nice shop and I took the time to call my mother.

I headed out on I-15 and saw the mountains I'd crossed yesterday in the distance. They sure looked nice and clear today. Oh well. I'll have to come back again. I was passing a lot of crops. I'm assuming they were potatoes, but I'm not sure as I've never seen potatoes on the hoof before. I take that back. PEI is covered with them. Yes, they must have been potatoes. It's the first time I've ever seen an extremely large farming apparatus trundling down the interstate. I couldn't begin to tell you what it was. I believe it had to do with farming because it was green and had "John Deere" written on it. The other fun part of driving in Idaho is that they haul the giant bales of hay on open trailers. I was driving along trying to figure out why there was so much straw blowing around when I came upon my first one. I saw these huge bales of hay in the fields in South Dakota and Wyoming. Now they're going to market.

I hit 3,000 miles on my trip today. It was just outside of Twin Falls, ID. I was heading to the dealership there for a couple of reasons. I really needed another shirt. I didn't make great choices when packing. I was also hoping for some kind of vented jacket I could wear to keep the sun off of me while remaining as cool as possible. The only one they had was black. When I'm trying to stay cool, I'm not thinking black. I did finally find a t-shirt. It has a nice design with the saying, "Too Fast for Love." LOL Don't worry. I don't think I'm that cool. The saying can be roughly translated as, "I'm 45 and still haven't figured out what I'm looking for."

It was about that time it started getting hot again, and I was headed for the Nevada desert. Nothing like a lot of sand and rocks to make you feel cool on a hot summer day. Right. I stopped at a small convenience store somewhere in Idaho just north of the Nevada border on US 93. While standing around in the air conditioning swigging a large bottle of PowerAde, I saw a notice on the wall about some local wildland fires. Since it was printed for today, I assume they print one every day. They have a summary of the local fires, with statistics for size, containment, number of personnel working on the fire, cost of the fire, etc. I asked the cashier a question about it and she had me speak to another store employee who happens to be a commissioner for the fire district. These fires are just outside his district, so except when they need mutual aid, his crew hasn't responded. We talked a bit and it was interesting to learn a little about the world of wildland firefighting. After leaving the store I noticed some of the fires burning in the distance. I thought about how these firefighters, who would be considered "call men" in New Hampshire (paid, but not a regular salary), are out there in this oppressive heat, with the heat of the fire on top of that, climbing mountains and doing intense physical work. You really have to give those men and women a lot of credit.

There was this short burst of odd landscape in Nevada. Imagine piles of sand. Now imagine that the grains of sand are 10 foot wide boulders. It looked like there were these piles that someone had scooped up and left there, but they were very large rocks. It was too hot to stop and take a picture. The rest of the ride was uneventful. It was hot. 100 degrees, but it was much more tolerable than it had been on the plains in South Dakota. The terrain was mostly sage brush (I assume) and sand, but at one point I came across a small crop with one of those big watering contraptions. The device was well off the road, but when I drove by it, the temperature dropped 10 degrees. It was a very pleasurable 4 seconds. It's amazing how that bit of water being sprayed made such a difference in the temperature around it.

I'm in a hotel again. This time camping wasn't even an option. I can't recall a sign for a campground since I've been in the state. It's funny how the lower the price of the motel, the better my wireless connection. My theory is that the cheap hotels will be less likely to have guests with laptops all fighting for bandwidth.

Tomorrow is the big day! I arrive in California. Previously I wasn't sure if I really wanted to go to the coast because I'm not hitting the Atlantic coastline. Then I remembered that I am stopping by the Jersey Shore on the way home, so I'm determined to visit the Pacific coast, if only for a quick photo.

SUNDAY, JULY 29, 2007

3301 - 3503 Arrived!

A short ride, but it started off with a little drama. Of course you can't have a good story without any adversity, so it isn't all bad.

I don't think I mentioned previously about the oil issue I had on the day I was hanging out with Darryl and Matt, the guys I met in Wyoming who are from Ohio. I suspect that it started that morning when I checked my oil and might not have been very forceful when I put the dipstick back in. At any rate, when we arrived in Tensleep, I noticed that oil had spewed out of the tank, all over... well, all over everything behind it. Needless to say, the oil level was a little low. I bought a quart of synthetic oil and poured most of it in. In the past, when the oil tank has been filled to the full level indicated on the dipstick, it will seep out around the dipstick while riding. So, I usually keep it about a half quart low. I didn't do it this time, so logically there was some leakage. I didn't think much about it, since it was filled as indicated and this was nothing new. The guys thought the dipstick wasn't fitting tightly enough. I tried to get one in Cody, but the dealership there is really just a t-shirt shop. Life went on and I didn't think about it again.

Until Saturday morning. This was three days after the Tensleep incident. I went to start my bike and I felt something hitting my inner thigh. Hmmm. I moved my leg and tried to crank the bike again. The dipstick shot out of the oil tank and landed in the parking lot. Huh? I put it back in, tried again, same result. I didn't go for a third time. I called the Harley dealership in Reno. Thankfully the service department was open early. We discussed and they felt there might be too much oil. Considering the events of days prior, it made sense. Why it didn't do it before that? I don't know. I'm extremely thankful that this happened on start up in the cool part of the morning and not while I was tooling down the road. I imagine I would have felt the hot oil spattering against my leg, but it wouldn't have been good. They also mentioned that the dipsticks with the temperature gauges in them don't fit as tightly as stock. That particular dipstick is the very first accessory I bought for my bike. It's been in there over 6 years and 60,000 miles. Could be it's the end of its life.

I dug out my tools and of course I didn't bring the 5/8" socket I had contemplated bringing for my oil change. A custom Harley had just pulled into the hotel parking lot and I asked the rider if he had the socket I was looking for. He pointed to his buddy's bagger, which had an opened tool kit sitting on the seat. Sure enough, there was a 5/8" socket. The guy pulled an old coffee cup out of the garbage can and I proceeded to drain about 8oz of oil from the bike. The tech had also suggested taping it shut, so I went across the street to the convenience store and bought a small roll of duct tape. Done. Cranked it up; dipstick stayed put. Problem not quite solved, but worked around for the time.

I got on the road and made it to the dealership. No stock dipstick. Oh well. It was working. I picked up the stuff I need for my oil change on Monday. My plan was to get to Marsha's in Truckee around noon. This was the original official destination. I got there at 12:45. Not bad for an 8 day, 3500 mile trip.

When I crossed into California, I started crying. It took me completely by surprise. While I've been very excited about the trip and feel it's an extraordinary adventure, I haven't felt sentimental about it. Steve said I was doing it to prove something. It never occurred to me that I couldn't do this. I'm not climbing Mount Everest. I'm riding a motorcycle across the country. Fun, exciting, but not an amazing feat. However, when I crossed the line, it wasn't just that I'd made it to California. I made it from giving birth to a child while living in the woods with a psycho husband and no electricity and running water, to raising an amazing son on my own, earning an Associate's degree, a Bachelor's degree, and recently an MBA. I was able to buy the motorcycle back in 2001 and now have a great job where I could take the time off to do the trip. It wasn't just a trip across the country, it was having nothing and being in dire circumstances and working my ass off to make life better. I arrived.

TUESDAY, JULY 31, 2007

3503 – 3977 Day trip to the coast

Wrote this last night in my tent. I'm a day behind. Sorry to worry everyone. The last two days have been AWESOME! More udpates later...

As long as I've come this far, I might as well make the Pacific coast. It would have been great to take some of the scenic roads around that part of California, but if I wanted to get to the coast and back in one day, I needed to blast through on the Interstate. The plan was to take I-80 all the way to the Bay Bridge, go down to the waterfront, cross the Golden Gate Bridge, stop at the Harley dealership in Corte Madera to see if they had a dipstick, and head back pretty much the same way.

I jumped on I-80 in Truckee, heading up Donner Pass. The road sucked. I've since learned that California roads universally suck. It probably didn't help that this was a portion of road where chains are required for trucks under certain weather conditions. It appears that the chains have dug these ruts in the road surface. I say "road surface" because I'm not sure exactly what it was. It looked like a big mosaic – rocks set in concrete. Add to that the unrelenting patches, holes, cracks, etc. It would have been fine if all I had to worry about was keeping the shiny side up.

I have this issue with my saddlebags. It's a love-hate relationship. I have detachable, locking, hard, painted-to-match. I love that they lock. I love that they have the same paint as my bike and look good. The part I'm not crazy about is the detachable feature. They have been known to detach at will – and not my will. After much angst, it was determined that they were randomly detaching because I had axel nut covers installed on my bike, and when I hit big bumps, the tabs that hold the bags to the brackets were hitting the axle nut cover, bending up, and the fasteners holding the bags to the brackets was not enough to hold the bag on there. I took the covers off. The bags have not yet separated completely from the bike since this modification was made, but the tabs that are supposed to slip over the bottom of the brackets have a tendency to bounce off their mount on a good bump. Sometimes I've found the bags holding on with just one of the fasteners still attached. I continually remount the bags and bend the tabs back around the bracket, as I was told to do by tech support, but the tabs don't seem to give a rat's ass what I want them to do.

The problem with losing a bag is that the coefficient of friction between pavement and the saddlebag is fairly high. Paint is scraped off as well as actual saddlebag material. The first time the bag fell off I used it as an excuse to have the bike painted. The second time it fell off I paid $250 to have the thing fixed and repainted. It probably comes as no surprise that National Cycle takes no responsibility for this cost. I was lucky on both of these occasions because I was riding on rural New Hampshire roads and I was able to stop, pick up the bags with the contents intact, and reattach them. Now, imagine if one of those babies fell off while I was driving down I-80 in California traffic. Whatever was in them (pocketbook, expensive camera, MacBook) is no longer going to be in one piece if I am lucky enough to ever gain custody of the items again. So I was a wee bit anxious pounding over this hard top logging road at 70 miles per hour.

I called Missy, who lives somewhere around Sacramento, when I stopped to eat some breakfast. She was looking at directions online while I looked at my map. I found a good route to get to her area and told her I'd be there in 30 minutes. Yeah. I guess if that had been a perfectly straight line between the two big lines on the map, that would have worked. It was only about 7/16" long. The space between the two big lines that is. If you were to straighten out that line, it would have been a couple of inches. Beautiful road – route 49 between I-80 and US 50. Very twisty, mountains, wimpy drivers that wouldn't use turnouts. I didn't check the time, but I'm sure I was over an hour.

It was great to chat with Missy for a while before I headed out. She wanted to get a picture of us together before we parted ways. There was a biker with a Vietnam Veterans patch sitting outside at a table. I told him I'd just ridden my bike across the country and we'd really appreciate it if he'd take a picture of us together since we'd probably never see each other again. He was more than happy to help and asked where I was heading. He was concerned about some races or other stuff going on that would make the Bay Bridge difficult. He suggested a northern route, which worked well with my plans.

Coming over the mountain into the Bay area was spectacular. It was a little tough to see too much while driving, but I had plenty of time to see it all as I got close. It had been hot inland, but the air cooled considerably as I approached the coast. I crossed the Richmond Bridge and went on to the dealership. There wasn't much at the dealership. They didn't have any dipstick that would fit my bike. I thought I'd check out the t-shirts because I assumed that a store called Golden Gate Harley-Davidson would have a great custom back that would look good in my quilt. Nope. I left the dealership and called Dudley Perkins to see if they could help me.

The parts guy gave me detailed directions and checked on the part, which he had in stock. I headed out across the Golden Gate Bridge. Wow. It has its own weather pattern. Remember that part in the Star Trek movie where they're at the Golden Gate Bridge and trying to talk to the whales so the weather will clear up and Earth won't be destroyed? I can see where that idea came from. It wasn't that bad, but before I knew it I was in the clouds, which were rapidly drifting across the road. It was clear for the crossing. It's like the bridge itself is a park. People are running and walking and riding bicycles across the bridge on the walkways. A much different feeling than any of the Hudson River crossings. The view of the city was awesome, and the view on the right side was just water – I was on the coast.

Getting to the dealership was quite a bit tougher than I expected. I felt like I was approaching a panic attack at one point. It's tough being in a very large city, 3500 miles from home, on a motorcycle, in tons of traffic, and not knowing where you are going. When I got to the American Airlines cargo warehouse at the airport I stopped to call again. I finally found it. Great store, great people, I got what I went there for.

The ride back to Truckee was long and it got dark about the time I was hitting the 80 mile long high-speed logging road portion of the road. I was happy to see the full moon rising. While it didn't help too much with the road, I was able to see the silhouette of the mountains and the light reflecting off Donner Lake when I came over the pass. I got to the house at 10:30; a long day, but my motorcycle saw the Pacific for the first time.

3977 - 4305 Heading back east

It was nice to have a leisurely breakfast with Marsha and her boyfriend in the morning. Leisurely for me, anyway. I forgot that it was Monday morning and most people were getting up for work. We looked at the map and wrote out a route and off I went. Right off I got screwed up and ended up at Lake Tahoe way below where we had planned.

When I hit King's Beach I'd been driving for almost an hour. I was mortified and thought that I'd been driving around in circles. Then I realized what I had done.

Mt. Rose Highway was beautiful and I got a view of Lake Tahoe from way above the lake. After that I headed down 341 towards Virginia City (think Bonanza). Amazing road. Fun curves and great scenery. I stopped in Virginia City to take a look around. Very touristy. Then on to Fallon for an oil change at the home of one of the guys from the Bike Talk forum. That was some dirty oil. I was nervous about the next part of the trip, Hwy 50 through Nevada. It's called the Loneliest Road in America. I can see why. The first town is 112 miles away.

Before this trip, I thought of desert as lots of sand, sand dunes, maybe some cactus. I've been through a lot of desert on this trip, but it's much different. More like hills and mountains with sage brush. No grass; not a lot of trees. At one point there was a short stretch of highway with landscape that looked like mounds of giant pebbles. Then I saw this huge sand dune. It was an enormous pile of sand - just like you'd expect in a desert. Turns out it is Sand Mountain. It was hard to tell just how big it was until seeing vehicles parked around the bottom of it. Amazing. This part of the ride ended up being one of my favorite parts of the trip so far. The road is lonely. There is very little traffic on it. I'll always call it Serenity.

I was taking it easy so I wouldn't burn too much gas. A couple of guys on Harleys passed me during that part, and I ended up running into them at the gas station in Austin. We chatted for a while. They are from the San Francisco area and one of them was born in Hanover, the next town to where I live.

I ended up at a small RV park in Eureka, Nevada, which was the next town past Austin, about 75 miles east. I got a patch of grass for the tent. There had been showers throughout this part of the trip, but they felt good. It was like swimming at 75 miles per hour. There were some showers while I was setting up camp, but I got it done and got settled down for the night.

4305-4780

Woke up early at the campground, packed up, and went back into town for gas and breakfast. I then got back on the road. The plan was to get to Salina, UT. For some reason I only had 300 miles planned for the day, and based on the mileage I'd been making, I was sure I'd make it farther. It was another hot day in the desert, but the scenery was well worth it. I stopped in Ely and called the dealership in Grand Junction to see if they'd be able to change my rear tire in the next day or so. No problem. Just bring it by and they'd get right to it.

I kept on and soon crossed into Utah. I was passing a gas station near the border. Right after the station was a sign that said it would be 83 miles until there would be more gas. Not sure why they don't put the sign before the gas station. I turned around and stopped to fill up. I asked someone where the state line is. He was standing on it! They have a yellow line painted across the parking lot to mark the boundary.

I made it to Delta, UT and stopped for gas and lunch. While I was eating, one of the guys I met at the gas station in Austin came in. We chatted for a while and then they asked if I wanted to ride with them. John's exact words were, "We ride fast and we don't shower every day, but you're welcome to ride with us." OK, maybe not exact, but something to that effect. I told them that I would, and if I didn't feel like keeping the pace I'd let them know and drop back. I cranked my bike and was waiting for the guys. My bike was doing that great classic Harley idle chant and John hollered over to compliment the sound. I yelled back, "That's carbureted, baby! You don't get that with fuel injection."

It didn't take long before I realized I wouldn't be able to keep up. My carburetor was gagging at 80 miles per hour. I pulled up next to John, pointed to my bike, gave the universal sign for choking and dropped back. When I got up to the next intersection, probably about 10 miles up the road, Terry and John were waiting for me. Once again, "That's carbureted, baby!" Good and bad. The guys were so sweet. They told me to lead the way and they'd put up with my measly 75 mph. The ride through Utah on I-70 was incredible. Every time we took a turn or came up over a rise, the scenery would take my breath away. My jaw would drop — literally. There were distance views and there were times when I felt like we were riding in the Grand Canyon. Unbelievable. I can't get over what a beautiful country we have. I knew that, but I didn't realize just how much of it there is out here.

We made Moab, got dinner and hotel rooms. Three separate rooms, by the way, for anyone thinking about turning this into a romance novel. John and I met at the hot tub and had a deep conversation about our higher power. They were both in AA. Terry was all set in his beliefs, but John, like me, just wasn't feeling it. We wanted to, but we weren't. After the hot tub was root beer floats at the Denny's next door. We decided that life just doesn't get any better than this.

THURSDAY, AUGUST 2, 2007

4780 – 5053

The plan was to go to the Arches National Park and then head to Grand Junction. I'd get my tire changed and the guys would go on their way to Sturgis. I was thinking the park would be a quick run in, look at the arch, and we'd be on our way in half an hour. That wasn't how it worked. It was one of those times when there is so much to see, so many pictures to take. Terry had been there before a few times and started saying that we were like kids running around and getting into everything. That's when we started calling him "Dad." Four hours later we left the park and headed back into Moab for lunch and to fill the tanks.

We started heading out of town through the canyon road, but a sign said the bridge was out so we went back the way we came. I ended up taking the lead on the way back to the interstate. We had the lane to ourselves. Soon John rode up next to me. When we had a passing lane, Terry came up on the other side and we rode three abreast for a couple of miles. I laughed and hollered at John that we were the three musketeers. Just more fun on another great day.

It wasn't too long before we made it to Grand Junction. The dealership was right off the interstate and was easy to find. Unfortunately it wasn't quite as easy to get in for a tire change as I was told over the phone. Apparently it's a big stop for Californians on their way to Sturgis. I wasn't given an answer as to whether they would even be able to get me in that day. Because of what I was told the day before, I wasn't too happy about it. I thought about going to Durango, but when I called there I was told it was first come, first served, and if I wanted to be in and out, I should be there at 7:30 the next morning. There was no way I was going to make it to Durango that day, so things weren't looking good.

Now it was a toss up between sticking around for a couple of hours to see if they could squeeze me in or getting back on the road immediately and waiting until Albuquerque. John was indignant when I told him what was going on and said I should speak with someone. I didn't think there was anything that could be done. A store employee asked what was going on and I told him. He suggested I speak with the owner and pointed me in that direction. I told the owner what I had been told the day before and that they were now unable to let me know if they could even get to it. He made a call and they got me right in. I felt like a jerk. I wouldn't have said anything, but I'm glad I did. They knew they were going to be busy; they should have said that over the phone. But, it all turned out very well.

While I was waiting, one of the salesmen went over my route from Grand Junction to Albuquerque with me. He told me where to get gas and where the hotels and campgrounds would be. I bought a shirt for myself and a patch for the t-shirt quilt while I waited. I also sat outside and wrote for the blog. I even had Internet access while sitting outside the building. When the bike was done, someone from service came out to talk to me. I expected the guy to be short with me, considering the circumstances, but he was very professional and apologized for the miscommunication. If he was thinking "bitch", he hid it well. He told me that the tech had found some fluid around the pads and was concerned about a leak. I figured it was oil from the dipstick fiasco of days before. So, new tire and axle nut (due to getting beaten by the saddlebags, I'm sure), and I was on my way. That is after I chatted with a couple of Vietnam Veterans for a while and thanked them for their service. They really appreciated that. I've turned into a regular social butterfly. I think I'm just having so much fun that I can't help myself.

I headed out towards Durango, noticing that I'd be dodging thundershowers along the way. It's interesting when you can see the weather for such a distance. I travel along a road without the knowledge of which way the road might turn, so I'm never sure if I'm heading into that big black cloud with random bolts of lightning, which in this case I had three different chances of hitting. After several turns towards and away from the various threats, I made it to the KOA campground just before Ouray.

The campground had an area designated as motorcycle camping, and there were several tents in the area. I figured there were a few separate groups until one of the guys started asking me about my trip. We spoke for a while and it turned out that there were 12 of them that were on an annual trip together.

The campground was really dark at night. Every time one of the guys from the group next to me went to the bathroom, they'd trip over my fire ring with a loud "bong." When it happened the third time, I couldn't help but laugh. One of the guys came over and invited me over to their campfire. I was assured that they were all good guys. Yeah. Not sure why I would believe that line, but I did. I guess it was my new social tendencies. They were great. Each one was introduced by his name, profession, and marital status. Not all of the 12 were there at first – or at any time really. A few had gone off on their bikes and hadn't returned. Others were snoring in their tents. I should mention that it was an eclectic group of motorcycles. Cruisers, sport bikes, touring, Japanese, American, and probably others. As much of a mix as you could get in 12 bikes, they had it. I felt like I was being interviewed by these guys, but it was fun being the center of attention and I didn't feel the least bit uncomfortable or out of place. They were perfect gentlemen and there were a lot of laughs. I was surprised to learn that one of the guys is a pastor and another is a worship leader. I have no idea what a worship leader is, but I'm sure it's something church related. I expected there'd be talk of God or some preaching going on, but that wasn't on the agenda for the night. I keep thinking of the noise of a fire ring getting kicked in the dark and I grin. Ken, Stephen, Dana, Dwight, Steve, Jay and the rest... another group of new friends I'll never forget.

FRIDAY, AUGUST 3, 2007

5053 – 5344

I got up, packed up, and had breakfast at the campground's café with the guys from northern Colorado. Then it was time to head out. I was told that the next stretch of road, the Million Dollar Highway, was going to be fun and scenic. It was all that. I spent a lot of time stopping to take pictures, but I also got a lot of good riding in. I probably would not have noticed the lack of guardrails on the sharp curves on the sides of cliffs had I not been warned. I try to keep it between the lines, regardless of road shoulder features.

As I headed up into the mountains, I thought of all the people I've met over the last two weeks. I have not felt threatened or feared for my safety at all. Between the stunning scenery and the genuine people this country has to offer, I feel as though my faith in everything has been restored - and that I now have faith where none existed. 15 years after getting sober, and I finally had the spiritual awakening (as they call it in AA) I'd been hoping for. I found God on the Million Dollar Highway.

The highway goes up into the Rockies. At one point the altitude is over 10,000 feet! That's a lot for an Eastern girl. Speaking of being an Eastern girl, have I mentioned how scaly I've become? These Westerners can gloat about their dry heat, but my skin likes amphibious New England. And dry heat? Yeah, that definitely makes me feel better when it's 110 degrees – not! I should say that it wasn't helping too much at first, but when I was leaving Grand Junction and sitting at a traffic light I estimated the temperature to be around 90 degrees. Just after that I saw a bank thermometer that proclaimed 104 degrees. Maybe there is something to it.

Anyway, at 10,000+ feet, I lost my rear brakes. Not totally, but I could barely reach as far as the pedal was going. I've been battling with this thing for a month now. They bled the line back home. I had bought brake pads thinking I needed new ones. I didn't, but I brought them along with me in case I needed them on the trip. They didn't find anything wrong with it at Sioux Falls. Considering Grand Junction's concern about fluid around the rear caliper, I figured I had a slow leak and planned to stop at Durango H-D when I got there. Of course these were the people who said there was going to be a line for service, but I still had some brakes, and if I needed to wait until Farmington or Albuquerque, that would be OK.

After more beautiful scenery and photo opportunities, I got to Durango and found the dealership. No problem. We'll take it right in. Great! After a while I learned that the tech recommended new brake pads. Fine. I've got 'em right here. Been packing and unpacking them for the last two weeks. Please, put them on. Then it was a new front tire. Yep. I knew that was coming. Go ahead. After a couple of hours I learned that there was nothing wrong with the brake line, it's just that if there are any bubbles in the line at all, altitude will expand them. That would explain the sudden loss in the pass. Not happy about all the money spent on maintenance in the last two days, but I do have two brand new tires and new rear brakes. That's what happens when you ride.

After leaving Durango I passed into New Mexico. I could see some thunderstorms in the distance, but as I've mentioned before, I have no idea how to tell if I'm going towards them. Coming into a small town called Aztec, it became very clear that I was headed right into one. I pulled into a gas station to wait for the storm to pass. I grabbed some ice cream and a Bingo scratch off lottery ticket to kill time. A lightning strike took out the electricity. The clerk locked up the store and I sat there with another customer until the storm moved on. I have to say I was a little uneasy being locked in a convenience store with no electricity or telephone. What better time to rob one? Maybe the register wouldn't open. I don't know, but I was happy when the storm passed. It was still raining a little so I put my rain gear on. About half a mile down the road construction started. That was some mean scored road. Very deep grooves. Then add mud and a lot of water. Pleasant.

I was able to get gas in Bloomfield and get back on the road. It turned into a nice, hot, sunny day before too long. I blasted on down the road toward Albuquerque, arriving at the hotel and happily getting settled for a few days. In fact, I'm staying an extra day here and cutting most of Texas out of the plan. I'll be going straight across I-40 to Memphis, which will give me back the extra day I'm spending here.

5344 - 5364

That's right. A whopping 20 miles so far today. I'm having a vacation from my vacation. I woke up at 9:00 and didn't get out of bed, except to travel to the bathroom, until after noon. That never happens. I guess I needed the break.

My 20 miles came from a trip to the nail salon, the local dealership for my t-shirt quilt material, breakfast/lunch (around 4:00pm), and a trip to the drugstore to stock up on (mostly) hair care items. I should have done the corn rows. I don't think I can possibly break this new comb. I hit the pool, did some reading and am now getting ready to go out to dinner with Samantha and her husband. He's been held up at work, so it's a little late, but since I had breakfast/lunch at 4:00, that's fine with me.

SATURDAY, AUGUST 4, 2007

5364 - 5530

After I wrote yesterday, I rode over to Samantha's house and we went out to dinner. I finally got to meet her husband afterwards. He had to work late and couldn't make it. I enjoyed the short ride back to the hotel from their house. It's been a while since I've ridden through city streets at night and I enjoy it. It was peaceful, and you don't have to worry about large animals stepping into your path, and everything has an interesting tint through the yellow-lens night riding glasses.

I got up at a reasonable hour this morning and eventually headed back over to their house. We were going to a Feast Day at a pueblo somewhere north of Albuquerque. When we got there, or I should say near there, the line of traffic stretched out so long, well we couldn't tell how long it was. We decided to bag it and headed for Santa Fe instead. The weather was perfect.

We got to Santa Fe and rode into the historic/tourist district. We parked the bikes and walked around the area. We did a little shopping with the street vendors and had lunch. We walked around some more and decided to leave. We stopped at the dealership on the way out and were unimpressed. The cheapest t-shirt was $25, and that was for black. If you wanted a color shirt it was $29. Who does that? I bought a patch to go on the t-shirt quilt.

The ride back was nice. We got off the interstate before Albuquerque and took some back roads. We went through a small town called Coralles. It looked like a storybook New Mexico village. There were some dark clouds heading towards Albuquerque. We assumed we were going to get wet and headed back. I had told Samantha that I wanted to get cowboy boots while I was on the trip, so we went to a big store and I found a pair of boots I love and a pair of jeans that fit. I brought three pairs of jeans with me. Two are too big and one is black and a little snug. I'm glad everything still fits the way it did when I left, but I feel like such a slug in the huge baggy jeans. I came back to the hotel from there and plan on resting up for another fun day in New Mexico tomorrow.

5530 - 5702

Today was another Albuquerque day. This time we added a couple more of Albuquerque's finest to the mix and headed to the mountains. Samantha's husband George chose to go with a long sleeve white shirt to limit the sun exposure. I mention this for a reason, which I'll get to later. The rest of us decided to risk skin cancer, and we headed north towards the mountains.

I can't tell you how we got there, but we ended up in the Jemez Mountains north of Albuquerque. It was interesting how the landscape changed so radically in a short period of time. First it was regular Albuquerque - desert with mountains on the side. Then it became more mountainous, but more of that red rocky stuff than the kind of mountains I'm used to. After lunch, where I had these incredible veggie tamales (and after which I requested a local fundraiser-type cookbook from Samantha), we ended up at this place that was the crater of a volcano a long, long time ago. Now it's green and woodsy and nothing like I would expect New Mexico to look. There's a lottery to hunt for elk there. I got a lot more details, but since I'm not qualified to write about hunting, I'll pass. I like to shoot guns, but I wouldn't know what to do with an animal if I shot it. Anyway, we stood around there for a while, took a couple of pictures, and headed back down the mountain. We were all a little low on gas, especially the Sportster in the group, so it was a good thing we were headed downhill.

We ended up at a restaurant in Bernalillo and had a snack. We discussed taking a ride on the Sandia Tramway. Samantha won't go at all and was recruiting someone to ride with me. George agreed to be my chaperone and away we rode to the mountain. He and I got on the tram with a few other people. It was an impressive ride. I can see where someone who doesn't like heights would not do well at all on this ride. Heart failure would not be surprising. I took a bunch of pictures, of course.

When we got to the top, we got out and looked around. It had to be 30 degrees cooler up there. Ahhhhh. A few more pictures and then we went to get into line for the ride down. At this point, George and I were on top of the mountain and Samantha and the two other guys were waiting at the bottom. Well it was us and probably everyone else who had rode the tram to the top of the mountain that day. We had to wait a couple of trams before we could get on and go down. It was expensive, but definitely a "must see" for the area.

At that point we wrapped it up for the day and I went back to the hotel to find that, once again, they didn't bother to make up my room. I guess when you get your room for free because you've earned points, they don't go out of their way to do anything for you. Anyway, another great day in Albequerque - and my last.

MONDAY, AUGUST 6, 2007

5702 - 6143

I really dragged my feet leaving this morning. Packing, mailing, a real breakfast, talking on the phone... I didn't get on the road until 11:00. I was sad to leave Albuquerque, but I was also happy to get back on the road. It wasn't too hot starting out, but a jacket was not required. Thinking I already had plenty of good tan on my arms, I limited the sunblock to my shoulders and face.

It was quite a long haul out of New Mexico. There was nothing very eventful. I stopped in Tucumcari for gas and lunch. One would think that with all the billboards and promotion of the place for miles and miles, it would have been a little more impressive. I got gas and decided to go to the A&W so I could get a root beer float with lunch.

I don't think I've mentioned my new method for drinking on the road since I lost my Camelback on I-90 in South Dakota. I figured this out while riding across Hwy 50 in Nevada. I had bought a bottle of Gatorade that comes in the long thin bottle with the sport cap - or whatever they call it. It's a big green thing that twists to open but stays attached. I had stuck it under a bungee cord behind my seat and took off. I got thirsty and wanted a drink so I pulled it out. I could hold the bottle in my left hand, bite down on the top, and twist it open. No problem. Until I was done with it.

I'm fine driving down the road with one hand. I can ride through curves by pressing or lifting with my throttle hand. The one thing I can't do with one hand is down shifting. I need the clutch for that. But it wasn't an immediate problem; I had all the time in the world. Remember, I was on Hwy 50. That's the one with towns about 90 miles apart on average. I considered slowing down and chucking the bottle off the bike and then stopping and running back to pick the bottle up. I thought about holding it under my leg but had a vision of plastic melting onto the rocker box covers.

I finally thought to shove it between the risers. For those of you who don't know, the risers on my bike are two pieces of chrome covered steel that come out of the top triple tree and hold the handlebars in place. I'm not going into triple trees; hopefully you get the idea. With my windshield on, the bottle was held in place by the risers and rested against the windshield. Perfect! Not only did this work as a good place to store an empty bottle, but it has become the place to store my drink while riding.

Anyway... on to Texas. This is the first time in my life that I've ever been to Texas! I don't know what took me so long. As you might expect, it was really hot. In fact, I was getting toasted at this point. I made it to Amarillo and stopped at the Harley dealership to consider buying a white long sleeve shirt for about the tenth time this trip. I thought that with all the sun I'd had so far I would have been past a burn. Nope. My arms don't hurt, but they are red. I'm starting to think that I have some Native American blood that nobody's ever told me about. I never get tan. I just keep getting redder.

I considered a jacket with some mesh and zippers, but I couldn't justify the hundred bucks. I ended up with this white long sleeved t-shirt with a studded Texas flag underneath the studded bar and shield. Honestly, that was the best option. It was better than the studded flowers with Harley-Davidson written in studs. For the last two years I have had a really hard time finding a decent women's Harley shirt. Someone got the idea that we want studs and sparkly shit. WTF? There are still biker chicks out here who aren't Rodeo Drive shopper wannabes, OK? And the skulls are a little over the top too. And the diamond-studded sparkly skulls? Argh. Who thinks this shit up? So anyway, as I said, I ended up with a studded Texas flag on white. It's now a bug spotted, studded Texas flag, but it certainly did the trick and kept me cool while keeping me from continuing the slow roast. It was after that that I texted Samantha and told her that I understood George's choice in a long sleeve shirt now. I should have purchased one of those many miles ago.

I also told Samantha that I felt like such a poser. I was wearing my new cowboy boots, my new Wrangler jeans, my new shirt with the Texas flag, and now a bandana around my neck to keep the crosswind from beating up my neck so badly.

Because I left so late the sun was sinking. I made it into Oklahoma - another state I've never been in before today - and made a KOA just before 9:00. It's not a bad place. I was able to get a sandwich, chips and a drink for less than $4, then rushed into my bathing suit to jump in the pool before it closed. I'm close to the interstate, which is also Route 66, and a few minutes ago I found out that there's an airport with large aircraft landing nearby. Probably Oklahoma City. So the surrounding area isn't very quiet, but the campground is. I'm sure I'll sleep well and be up early for my long haul to Memphis and the Graceland Campground tomorrow.

On a side note...

The day I was riding to Red Lodge, Montana, I quickly glanced at an historic marker that mentioned I was passing the site of the Smith Mine Disaster. When I got to the hotel that night, I looked it up on the Internet. What really shocked me about it was that at a loss of 74 people, it is the 43rd worst in the United States. That's a huge number of people to lose at one time, and it's the 43rd worst..

I thought of it because I just read that there was a mine collapse in Utah, not far from where I was riding a few days ago. I hope everyone makes it out safely.

TUESDAY, AUGUST 7, 2007

6143 - 6728

I paid for my slacking yesterday with a 575+ mile ride today. It wouldn't have been so bad if didn't get so hot, but it is August in the south. Can't expect much different. It started off well. I wore the long sleeve shirt again. I stopped soon after I started to get some of those in-ear ear buds for my iPod Nano. I had the idea that those might work after riding with Samantha and George. I can't keep the regular ear buds in, but I figured that the ones you shove way in would work. Knowing I had a long day ahead of me, I thought it would be a good time to try. They worked! So I was rocking going down the highway. Singing and tapping my foot and sort of dancing as best as one can while riding - I'm sure anyone who saw me thought I was nuts, but I didn't care. I had to hook up the Powerlet to the battery cable so I could charge the Nano while I was riding.

At first I couldn't keep the thing in my left ear and I thought it might be because the wind was whipping the cord everywhere. I stopped and slid it down my shirt and tied the bandana around my neck over the cord as well. Worked great. So, as I'm trying to make Memphis, Paul Simon's "Graceland" starts to play. Not only am I trying to make Memphis, but I'm staying at the Graceland Campground, which is right across the street from Graceland. I can't get the song out of my head. "Graceland, I'm going to Graceland. Graceland, in Memphis, Tennessee..."

I can't remember at what point the temperature became unbearable, but I ended up taking off the long sleeve shirt. I couldn't take it anymore. On went the sunblock. There just isn't a whole lot to say about the day. "I have reason to believe, we all will be received at Graceland..."

If you remember back a couple of weeks, I mentioned that I had this vision of arriving back home looking like Forrest Gump after he ran back and forth across the country a few times. Well today was the day. Despite applying #70 SPF sunscreen over my entire face, my nose, especially the area around the sunglasses, is brownish/black. It's an odd color; not really tan. Just dark. My nose is peeling a little around the sides. My forehead's taken it hard too. In fact, it took a bug so hard today that when I wiped the guts off my forehead, it appears I took a layer of skin as well. I'm sure it was ready to peel anyway, but it seems that bug guts are an effective exfoliant. That would be the snot yellow variety of bug guts.

Then the sunblock I put on my arms after changing into a sleeveless shirt came to the surface on a layer of sweat. I couldn't have been more wet if I'd just emerged from a lake, with a white film over all of it. And the hair. Ahhh, yes. The hair. Imagine two pigtails coming straight down with pieces coming out at every level of braid. Think Medusa.

I went into a McDonalds to get something to drink. I was dying, or I would have died had I stayed on the road. My brain was baked and my mind was turning to mush. So I went into the McDonalds and I swear the cashier was terrified. I even scared a cop a little later. I think he was going for his gun until he realized I was smiling. "My traveling companion is 9 years old. He's a child of my first marriage. We're going to Graceland..."

OK, that's it for tonight. The bugs here are awful. I'm not fond of Graceland or Memphis, Tennessee at this point. Hopefully it will all be better in the light of day.

WEDNESDAY, AUGUST 8, 2007

6728 - 7131

I hate the east coast. I am now an official believer in dry heat. Two weeks ago I would have said it is a load of crap designed to make people feel better that they live in the desert. The Graceland Campground sucked. It might be just dandy if you're in an RV, but it is definitely not the place for tenters. Do I sound a little cranky? I don't want to go home!

I couldn't even put sunscreen on this morning because I was already drenched in sweat. I had to go into a convenience store and wipe myself down with my bandanna before I could put the stuff on. Let's see... today... tons of traffic, rode until my brain was baked and not functioning, stopped to cool down, rode until I was out of gas, stopped and filled up, rode until my brain stopped functioning, stopped and cooled down, ad nauseam.

Just so happened that Johnny Cash was playing on the iPod when I blasted through Nashville. I think that's the only country song I have. How appropriate. Oh, I also have On the Road Again by Willie Nelson. Got to have that song for the road. My goal was Tellico Plains, Tennessee. I was planning on staying at a new motorcycle campground here, but when I got there, nobody was there. Nobody. I turned around and came to another KOA. Very nice place.

I pitched my tent and jumped in the pool. There were a couple of swallows flying around. I was kicked back floating around the stairs in the pool and the swallows grew in number. Next thing I knew, they were diving into the pool for water. I could have reached out and grabbed some of the birds, they were so close. Very strange, but an interesting experience - a new one for me. Nothing much else. Looking forward to getting up early and riding the Cherohala Skyway and then the Tail of the Dragon, followed by another few hundred fast and hot interstate miles.

Have I mentioned that I don't want to go home?

THURSDAY, AUGUST 9, 2007

7131 - 7595 Tail of the Dragon

Today started off well. It was cool in the morning and it helped that there was air conditioning in the showers and bathroom at the KOA in Tellico Plains. I woke up just before dawn and got everything packed up. I stopped at the gas station just outside the campground to fill up before I hit the Cherohola Skyway. I decided to wash my windshield and noticed a huge crack and a hole in my headlight. It still worked, but probably not for long. I vaguely remember hearing something that worried me yesterday. Must have been it. Better the headlight than my eye.

As I suspected, I stopped constantly to take pictures. It was a little over 50 miles on that road to US-129, a portion of which is the Tail of the Dragon. Before the Dragon started, I passed a small motorcycle shop. I turned around and went back to Wheeler's and got the headlight and a couple of t-shirts. What a great place. Small, but all the important stuff. After looking at the website, I assume it was Ken Wheeler who helped me out. He was very friendly and had no problem with me replacing the headlamp in his parking lot. Some shops don't like that. I'm not sure why I can't do anything on my bike without requiring first aid, but I got the light in successfully with only a small amount of blood lost. He also had a bunch of stuff there for people to use - for free! For example, he had a can of that Plexus that Rocky used on my windshield back in Nevada, so I cleaned the windshield again.

It worked well on the turn signal lenses too. Anyway, I got it all taken care of and took off for the Dragon.

The road was good. It was a nice quiet morning. At first I had nobody ahead or behind me, which I liked. Nobody to hold me up, and nobody to make me feel rushed. Then I caught up to a couple of guys. Then a cop got behind me. It was still fun, but I had to hold back a little. Probably a good thing. I can't see going down there just for that road, but there are a lot of other good roads around there as well.

It was starting to get hot again as I finished. Looking at my HOG map, I thought it would be a good idea to go up 321 instead of 411. Not a great idea. That road takes you through Pigeon Forge and Gatlinburg. Lots of traffic, lots of lights, too much heat. I was going to take the road all the way to Johnson City but decided to hit I-40 instead when I got there. Unfortunately I hit it in the wrong direction. I had a feeling I wasn't going the right way and stopped to check it out. It was hot. There were busloads of teenagers around. I was cranky. Not pleasant. After drinking half a soda I jumped on the bike and headed back towards Knoxville.

I had a really tough time at this point. It was another one of those days when I couldn't stay steady. Gas, water, bathroom, gas, water, water, water. I kept pushing on, but it was brutal and I was hating myself. At one point I was falling asleep on the road. I don't know why. Just in a daze I guess. I stopped at a gas station with a Subway and got a drink and sat down for a while. Fortunately I got my second wind and got in a groove. I finally made it into Virginia and the ride became effortless.

After I got into Virginia there was a sign that for the next certain number of miles there was a Highway Safety Coordinator. I thought, "That's what they must be calling State Troopers in Virginia these days." Must be that some rich dude with connections didn't like the way a trooper spoke to him and now they changed the title for those patrolling the Interstates, and they were telling the public exactly where they were going to be doing it. That's no fun. Then there was a sign stating the different fines for different offenses that the Coordinators found one guilty of. It all seemed confusing. So is this like airport security? You drive through this certain area and the Highway Safety Coordinators randomly pick out vehicles to get inspected for... whatever. So then I thought about the Coordinator that would pull me over, and he'll be this really hot guy and maybe he'll need to frisk me. Yeah, I'm totally down with this whole Highway Safety Coordinator thing. That whole scenario was moving right along when I saw the third sign and realized it was a Highway Safety Corridor, not Coordinator. Duh. Well, that occupied about 10 miles of my time today. Dehydration can really mess up your brain.

I made it as far as I had planned. I'm at a KOA which is expensive and I hate the site, but it's a place to sleep and it has Internet access. I'm not sure why campsite owners feel like tenters prefer to sleep in sand and dirt. A nice soft patch of grass that tent stakes sink into easily is my choice. I think this will be my last camp out for the trip. I'm almost home. I decided tonight that I don't want to get stuck in rush hour traffic in Baltimore and Philadelphia, and then Friday afternoon Jersey Shore traffic, so I'm sticking to the mountains and hope to make Ossining, NY tomorrow night.

Kind of like a song that's stuck in your head, hopefully if I put this out there it'll get off my mind. Not sure why I was blindsided by Tennessee memories. Should have expected it. My son is half Tennessee hillbilly. The last time we were here was 6 years ago to bury his dad. Before that, closer to 20 years since I've been here. I was reminded of him when I stopped at a gas station in Arkansas and saw a guy from Tennessee on a bike. Clean cut guy, shiny new bike, shiny new patch. Same patch Buck wore when I met him. Things have certainly changed in 20 years, myself included.

FRIDAY, AUGUST 10, 2007

7595 - 8108

It's late. I just wanted to check in. I thought there wouldn't be any more stories to tell this close to the end, but I was wrong. Like I said before, you can't have a good story without adversity. Nothing like breaking down in the cold and rain a few hundred miles from home.

I got up early and packed up. It was a little foggy, but it was nice not having the sun beating down so soon. The plan was to go to Ossining, NY in Westchester County, but I would possibly be going to Debbie's a little farther upstate. I even considered trying to make it home if I made the Tappan Zee Bridge by 4:00. The fog and clouds stuck around for a little while, and I noticed that I'd barely missed some rain a few times. My lucky day!

I had gone over 250 miles when I stopped for an early lunch around 11:00, so I was optimistic about getting to the Hudson River by 4:00. The exit I stopped at for lunch had a Harley dealership, Appalachian Harley-Davidson, so I decided to stop by and see if they had any good t-shirt backs for the quilt. The custom back they had was OK, but their cheapest plain old t-shirt was $31! Forget it. I thought $29 was bad in Santa Fe and refused to buy there. Patches for both of them.

When I was getting ready to leave there, I decided to pull my cell phone out of the saddle bag and take it off the charger. I had a message from Debbie telling me that it had been pouring rain all day and there were no signs of the rain letting up. I had noticed that New Hampshire had been forecast for rain also. My hopes of getting home diminished, but I hadn't completely given up. The weather was perfect where I was at this point. Some of the best weather the whole trip. Sunny with a few clouds and just the right temperature for sleeveless riding. I got back on 78 and headed toward Allentown, PA. About an hour before the New Jersey border I hit a cool spot. I thought it was nice for a little spot, but if the temperature was like that consistently I'd have to put a coat on. The "spot" never ended. It was more like the edge of the cold front, so I stopped to put my coat on. It appeared I was getting into that rain soon too, so I pulled the rain gear out of the bag and made it handy.

The traffic got thicker and less courteous. No way! This is New Jersey I'm talking about. Who'd a thunk? I got on 278 going north towards New York and the humidity became a little more liquid. I stopped at a rest area to put my rain gear on. I was freezing too, so more clothing wasn't a bad thing. I called Debbie, who commented on my ability to find weather from one extreme to the other. 104 degrees one day, and it couldn't have been even 60 degrees at that point. I wasn't doing well as I got close to New York so I pulled off in Mahwah, NJ, just before some heavy traffic. After getting off the Interstate, I realized I'd made a bad exit choice. I had no idea how I was going to get back on and the backup was horrendous.

I finished my coffee and ventured out. I found the way back into the bumper to bumper mess that I was worried would be the entire 12 miles to the Tappan Zee. I was surprised that there was traffic going into Westchester, which is a Hudson River crossing that gets you on the Manhattan side. All the traffic should be heading out of the city and suburbs and into the countryside for the weekend. Fortunately the traffic was for I-87 and not 287 and while the road to the bridge was congested, it was not stopped. I always feel like I've arrived when I cross the Tappan Zee because of the trip from Georgia to New York that my son and I took 17 years ago. It was after 4:00 and I was clearly not making it to New Hampshire that day, but after riding over 8,000 miles, the bridge did give me the sense of coming home. It was short lived.

I stopped just over the bridge in Tarrytown for gas. Then I got back on 287 with the plan of getting on the Taconic Parkway to go to Debbie's. I wasn't sure of the exit, but I assumed there would be a sign since the Taconic is a major road between suburban New York City and Albany, the state capitol. I thought it was one of the first exits, but I hadn't seen a sign. I started thinking about the Parkway Vortex (my own term) in Westchester, which is around Hawthorne, where all the parkways come together. The Saw Mill crosses through this area on its route from 684 near Katonah to Manhattan where it becomes the West Side Highway. You also have the Sprain Brook Parkway and the Bronx River Parkway. You might think that the Bronx River Parkway is named that because it runs along the Bronx River. Not so. It actually becomes the river when it rains hard enough. Anyway, the Bronx River Parkway ends around there, and the Sprain Brook becomes the Taconic near the same spot as well. As I said, I was expecting to see a sign for the Taconic, but then I started sorting through where each parkway went (it's been a while since I've been in the area) because I might need to get on Parkway A to make it to Parkway B. By the time I'd figured it all out, I was well past the exit and pushing on towards 684 and Connecticut.

I was cold and frustrated and tired and feeling on the edge at this point. I decided to head up 684 and stop at the first exit to call Debbie and decide whether I should go to her house still or just try to make it home. Debbie said I hadn't gone too far out of the way and gave me new directions. At that point I was not in the mood to be riding anywhere. I was at the exit for the Westchester Airport. I turned around and headed back onto the Interstate. I hit a series of good potholes and the bike quit. First I thought gas, but I'd just filled up. Did I turn the gas on? I haven't turned it off the whole trip. Besides, all the indicator lights had gone out. As I was pulling over, I knew it was electric. I called Debbie as soon as I stopped. I hadn't been in a great mood five minutes before. It wasn't much better at this point. I told her I was going to pull my seat off and take a look.

Sure enough, the ground cable had snapped. Simple enough, if you have a spare battery cable and the tools. And it isn't raining and getting near dark. And there isn't a ton of traffic and airplanes roaring overhead. I had almost packed my 10mm wrench, which is required for the battery terminals, but assumed that if I had needed it, one would be available to me. Stupid assumption. New Rochelle was the closest dealership that was open. They had the part. I asked them if they had a 10mm wrench they would sell to Debbie as well. The guy puts me on hold to ask someone. He comes back and tells me that Harley's don't use metric sizes so they don't have one. This is where I lost it.

Last winter when I was taking my battery out for the season, I tried a couple of wrenches and nothing fit. I finally pulled out my service manual and discovered I needed a 10mm. I had to drive to

Sears and buy one. Seemed like a waste of time and money at the time and I've always been irked and perplexed that this is the case. So, being tired, wet, cranky and broken down - so close, yet so far away from home - and having this guy talk to me like I'd made the choice to have metric battery terminals... I went over the edge. Fucking Harley-Davidson and the fucking battery and the fucking New York roads and on and on. I apologized and they said they'd have the cable for me. Unfortunately there was no way Debbie could make it to New Rochelle before 8:00 when they were closing. The next time I spoke to her, her boyfriend was removing the ground cable from her Lowrider and they were bringing it down to me.

As I was standing on the side of the road (I was on the entrance ramp) and about a thousand cars had passed, I was wondering, where's a Highway Safety Coordinator when you need one. This would have been a great time for that guy to show up and rescue me. Instead it was Hugh Grant. Not really, but the guy looked just like him. I figured for someone that good looking to stop and help, he must be a serial killer. He tried his best, but there just wasn't anything he could do. He gave me his phone number and offered to loan us some tools if we needed them.

As it was getting dark, Debbie and Andy showed up with the battery cable. Andy put it on, the bike had power, and we were off. Poor Debbie. Her commute is bad enough as it is, but she had to drive over an hour home in the rush hour traffic just to turn around and drive all the way back to the equivalent of White Plains on a rainy Friday evening. What a great friend. I'm also very thankful that I didn't find the Taconic. That road is a corridor of death. I'd have ended up looking like one of the armadillos I saw roadside back in Texas. It could have been a lot worse in so many ways.

When we got back, Andy made us an incredible dinner (I guess he does that) and after a little talking it was time for bed. Today is supposed to be much nicer. What I have thought of as a full day's ride, from New Hampshire to suburban New York, is now a walk in the park. 250 miles? An easy morning ride - on the Interstate anyway. I'll probably go for a little more of a scenic ride before heading home to a mountain of mail.

SATURDAY, AUGUST 11, 2007

8108 - 8323 The home stretch

I wasn't in any rush to get home. I decided to take the Taconic north, then hop on 22 and cross over into Vermont. It was a record low temperature in New York this morning, but it was supposed to get up to 80. I packed up and hopped on the Taconic. I know I said bad things about the Taconic yesterday (corridor of death, I think my words were), but that's for the part south of I-84. It's a very nice road on the northern stretch; two lanes in each direction, no commercial vehicles, nice hills and curves, and scenic. The Highway Safety Coordinators were out in force. I've received a NYS trooper's autograph on that road before (actually, I've had his a couple of times, although I didn't tell him that) so I took it easy.

I was on the road for a few miles when I thought about an old friend that lives right off the parkway up closer to Albany. She's a good enough friend that I had no problem stopping by unannounced. I usually like to call first, but her number wasn't in my cell phone and I didn't think she or her husband would mind. I couldn't remember exactly where to get off the parkway, so I stopped for gas and checked out a map. Perfect! I just had to follow the road I was on and I'd be there in a few minutes. They were home and it was great to see them. I was surprised to learn that they now own a bar/restaurant in the neighboring town. Betsy was on her way to open up for the day, so I followed her in. What a great place! They have a volleyball net and horseshoe pits outside. It was very clean and comfortable inside. Betsy is probably the most friendly, fun and social person I know. She is perfect for that job and I'm sure they'll be very successful.

When I was there I remembered that my mother had told me she'd be in Canaan, NY that day. I determined that Canaan was the next town over, so I called her and got the directions. She was at her brother's wife's family's place.

I enjoyed myself there. Except for my mother and stepfather, nobody has been reading my blog, so I had the chance to tell lots of stories. I love telling stories. It was a lot of fun for me, and I think they enjoyed hearing about the tales from the road. We sat out in the gazebo and I talked while they ate lunch. After lunch we went out to the bike and lots of pictures were taken while I was getting ready to leave.

The rest of the ride went without incident. Route 22 in New York is a beautiful ride and there were lots of bikes out. I crossed over into Vermont and eventually got on 100 north, which goes to Route 4 just east of Killington. Route 100 is one of the best roads in Vermont for scenery and quaint towns. It wasn't overburdened with tourists surprisingly. Before too long I was approaching the New Hampshire state line and home. I know I've praised the west and not said a lot of great things about New England, but we do have beautiful country and great roads here. As much as I hated ending my trip, it was good to be back home.

I sat on the porch for an hour before I came inside. Mixed emotions about sleeping in my own bed and not wanting to be home. Thankfully all my preparation paid off. I came home to a clean house, the bills were all paid, and there was nothing I had to desperately take care of. I had the foresight to take my Netflix account off hold on the 8th, so there were two movies waiting for me when I got home. I went to the dealership this morning to see everyone and order a battery cable. I'm going for a ride this afternoon and will probably start on my new t-shirt quilt this evening. I'm getting accustomed to the fact that life is back to the same old daily grind. Well, I better wrap this up so I can go for that ride...

Epilogue

As soon as I got back to New Hampshire, I started looking for a job in Colorado. I moved to Colorado that December.

I have more friends in a short time than I've had my whole life. The riding is amazing, and I now have almost 120,000 miles on my bike. I've become self-employed, and my work is all motorcycle related. Nothing is consistent, and I worry about making ends meet, but I'm not selling my soul, committing to a corporation that offers very little in return.

As far as my family goes, I don't hate my brothers, but we aren't very close. I eventually realized it was my younger brother who tormented me the most. I know he was reacting to his own situation, but our relationship remains distant. I'm closer to my older brother, but we don't communicate much. My mother and I have become much closer. She went through some difficult times and ended up marrying a good man and has become close to his family. With her pressure of high society gone, we have a lot more in common.

She's helped me out a lot over the years, and I'm glad she didn't give up on me a long time ago. I'm sure a lot of mothers would have.

I now have a granddaughter who has Buck's features, the expressive eyebrows, and a no fear attitude. I adore her. She has lots of Harley shirts, and I've heard that when she hears a Harley going by, she dances and blows kisses.

The year my granddaughter was born, I rode across the country to see her. In the same trip, I went down to Georgia and saw some old friends. I was able to spend a couple of hours with a woman who knew Buck and me well. She understood what I'd been through, and after I left her place, I felt as though a weight had been lifted from my shoulders. I never knew if anyone understood what had happened. Intellectually, I knew Buck had been sick with a tortured mind, but my heart was hard. After leaving Georgia, I was finally able to grieve over our lost marriage, the loss of his sanity, and his lost life.

I've written criticisms of past loves. I've even been engaged once since I've been in Colorado, (three times since I bought my bike). I'm not blind enough to believe I'm faultless in any of these relationships. I'm broken, and I'm afraid the guys I've had relationships with since Buck have had to suffer because of that. I have a huge fear of being trapped. I don't hate men, and I don't intentionally hurt anyone, but I haven't healed. I'm not sure that I will. But that's OK.

I'm approaching twenty years sober as I write this. The freedom is amazing. Having God in my life has also done wonders for my soul. It's not as difficult and limiting as everyone thinks it is. It's religion that makes it hard, so I ditch the dogma and stick with the good stuff.

I'm glad you made it this far. I sincerely hope you got something out of the book, whether it is purely entertainment or the confidence to make a change. Thanks for reading my story.